# The Hero's Journey Guidebook

# The Hero's Journey Guidebook

## Mapping the Story of Your Life

## Ben Pugh

RESOURCE *Publications* • Eugene, Oregon

THE HERO'S JOURNEY GUIDEBOOK
Mapping the Story of Your Life

Resource Publications
An Imprint of Wipf and Stock Publishers
199 W. 8th Ave., Suite 3
Eugene, OR 97401

www.wipfandstock.com

PAPERBACK ISBN: 978-1-5326-0836-0
HARDCOVER ISBN: 978-1-5326-0838-4
EBOOK ISBN: 978-1-5326-0837-7

Manufactured in the U.S.A.                    NOVEMBER 15, 2016

Chapters 1:1–1:2 have been adapted from my "Have You Heard the Call?" *Methodist Recorder* (September 11, 2015). Used by permission.

Chapter 2:1 has been adapted from my "Getting Past Your Grumpy Old Troll," *Methodist Recorder* (February 2016). Used by permission.

To my mother.

# Contents

# Introduction

"...the unnarrated life is not worth living."[1]

WHAT'S TRUE? WHAT'S REAL? We can't agree anymore about what life means. We call this "postmodernity." It is a particular episode of our culture. The old verities are under threat. We have come to realize that even science cannot explain everything. This loss of consensus is, of course, not a permanent state of affairs. It has happened before: the Reformation, the Enlightenment. New definitions of reality are soon put forward but, for a while, everything seems to be up for grabs. For the generation or so of people that live through these big cultural shifts, some matrix has to be found that rescues them from the nihilism and anarchy that lies in wait. It was during just such a time—the early eighteenth century—that the modern novel came to birth.[2] We tell ourselves stories as a way of recovering a shared understanding of who we are and how we got here.

As with previous cultural reboots, no-one is sure of anything at the moment. The system is in the process of restarting, and has

1. Kearney, *On Stories*, 14.

2. Many consider Daniel Defoe's *Robinson Crusoe*, published in 1719, to be the first true novel. It has the characteristic elements of totally believable realism and a continuous linear narrative that later became so familiar.

been since the sixties. People are anxious. Many are risk-averse while others are adrenaline-junkies. Overall, we are witnessing a retreat from adventure, all compounded by an all-out siege on our culture from Jihadi terrorism. The anti-establishment, world-changing confidence of the Swinging Sixties, leading to the playfully postmodern Nineties, has given way to the pallor of the Post 9/11 world. It is starting to look as though we haven't even the courage to be fully postmodern any longer and modernity's prized ideals of regulatory control and secular peace have bounced back. It seems we can no longer stomach the dizzying freedoms of unprincipled relativism. Some things, after all, are just plain wrong. But an equally ridiculous moral certainty keeps taking hold with all the attendant witch hunts, allegations and scandals. The external threats seem to compound our war on each other.

But there is hope. Culture has an instinctive ability to rebuild itself around some new set of ideals. Two new ideals are emerging. Firstly, the new consensus is looking like it will be heavily committed to pragmatism. What works, and only what works, is true and valuable. In a world in which no single perspective on something can ever be final, such pragmatism is one of the only options left to us. Individually created truth is only of use to anyone else if tried and tested. This is perhaps most marked in the context of church. It is there of all places where we expect high principles and strong theoretical underpinnings. Instead, even the most fantastical ideas about the binding of territorial spirits are propagated because of anecdotes about how such methods have apparently worked. In the recent past, church growth conferences attracted huge numbers of disillusioned pastors of tiny churches in the hope that even a model from South Korea might work for them in Milwaukee. The challenge to everyone, if pragmatism is to dominate, will be how to let it rule us in a way that is dignified, visionary and creative rather than crass, unprincipled and utilitarian.

Community is the other main outcome of postmodernity. In a community, a tribe or a team, we all pool our perspectives in the hope of negotiating some degree of consensus. And so it is that TV and radio shows that would once have been hosted by one presenter are now presented by a team, a posse of jesting colleagues who all have a say. In universities we learn collaboratively, research reflexively and write multi-voiced. In our post-industrial world some experiment with leaderless organizations[3] and many try to reform our politics so that it is structured on a human scale: devolved and less bureaucratic[4]—and so we should. Please, more of that!

And as we gather to rebuild our fractured world, as we try pragmatism cemented by community, we tell stories. Stories provide the plan. Stories give the architecture of the world we are trying to build. Stories speak of life in a way that is not open to empirical experiment in any scientific sense yet they are profoundly pragmatic. Stories tell the community what works at a deep level, a level only decipherable by the community that owns them and tells them. These stories speak to the depths of our being in a way that nothing else could ever do. They are profoundly therapeutic: they rebuild relationships, they restore hope, they confirm common values.

In this book, we will be exploring the power of narrative using an adaptation of a particular matrix. Christopher Vogler, in his book of advice for screen writers, called it the Hero's Journey.[5] This is a structure, a story spine, that you can lay over your life as it looks so far. It is like a retrospective Sat Nav. At the moment, you look back upon your life and there are many roads and seemingly random changes of landscape. It is difficult to read. You're not sure what you're looking for, what you should pick out that shows you the path you have taken, why you have taken it and where it is leading if you stay on it. The Hero's Journey matrix will, like a Sat Nav, illuminate the roads that matter. It is my hope that as you read, you will reflect upon your life and find that the path and its trajectory become clear. I hope also that you will begin to see that

---

3. See the fascinating book by Frederic Laloux: *Reinventing Organizations: A guide to Creating Organizations Inspired by the Next Stage of Human Consciousness.*

4. I am thinking of David Cameron's efforts in the direction of a Big Society.

5. Vogler, *The Writer's Journey.*

your life makes sense as a life that God cares about; that you will begin to see where he has interjected and called you in some way to some particular adventure or series of adventures.

The main ideas of the Hero's Journey originate from the pen of a mythologist called Joseph Campbell. His book, *The Hero with a Thousand Faces*, first came out in 1949. The whole idea is of a hero and his adventurous journey into some cavernous underworld to obtain the secret of everlasting life for everyone else. This basic story line is, according to Campbell, so pervasive in human cultures that he refers to it as the "monomyth." In other words, there is really only one myth, many variants. Campbell's insights were popularized via Vogler's *The Writer's Journey* to become a hugely influential way of both analyzing and helping to create the great stories of Hollywood. *Star Wars* was soon analyzed in this way, and Vogler himself was invited to analyze the storyboard for *The Lion King* while it was still being written. His input helped to give the baboon Rafiki a more meaningful role as Timon's Mentor.

Today, any Google search will reveal just how many blogs there are out there advising screen writers and novel writers on how to use this model. It has become almost ubiquitous largely because, as Campbell claimed, it is a structure which already underlies all the great myths of human history. Writers use it to help them pick out what is latently already there in the tales they are creating. This is perhaps why it is such a strong model: it merely picks out and identifies more clearly the elements that tend to turn up in any given story. Writers produce these elements unconsciously because they are already the kind of stuff that life is made up of.

What I am doing here is simply applying this template to real life from a faith perspective: analyzing real life stories of faith in the same way that screen writers analyze made-up stories to help bring out more clearly the things that life is really made of. This, I hope will help us analyze our own stories to discover a divine purpose in them.

The reason for the appeal of fictional stories is that they speak to us, and they do this so well because we see ourselves in them. In that sense, fiction is true. Jesus himself knew this as he spoke of the

Kingdom of God in made up parables. Fiction is more true than life itself because it hints so strongly at the answers to our "why?" questions. Fiction tells us the meaning of life in a very immediate, intuitive way. This is what I hope *The Hero's Journey Guidebook* will do for you as we explore the model in relation to real life in the same way that it has been explored in relation to made-up life.

Following Vogler, I'm giving your life's adventures a three act structure: a short beginning, a long middle and a short end. Within Act 1 is your call to some particular action and your initial response. In Act 2, assuming you rise to the call, however falteringly, you face your ordeal, your test, out of which you emerge a better person with your priorities right and your deepest needs met. Towards the end of Act 2, there is a decisive battle. You win the fight. This results in Act 3, the journey back. In Act 3, there are still some obstacles to overcome but, basically, you are now on your way to living happily ever after. I will illustrate all of this with the stories of those that have travelled this way before.

You are probably right now coming to the end of one adventure, as well as being at the beginning or middle of another adventure. There is often some overlap. Recognizing such an overlap is a useful coping mechanism as it means that you can take courage from the great victories you are winning in one area of your life while you face the more difficult earlier stages of another adventure.

I am anticipating that many of my readers have picked this book up because, in their hearts, they want to follow Christ more authentically. This is not to exclude those who may be only exploring faith in God, but, to help with the desire to follow Christ, I have offered suggestions right at the end of each chapter about how the Hero's Journey motif might be indexed to the life of Christ. Interestingly, not all of it can, and that despite Campbell's original claim, which he does not adequately support, that the story of Christ is basically the same as that of every other mythical hero. There is no way, for example, to tie any episode from the four canonical Gospels into the Ordinary World, though this is, admittedly, part of Vogler's adaptation and only implied in Campbell's original version. But neither do we find Christ being "called" to his adventure within the Gospels, though clearly we could shoe-horn a Call in somewhere if we tried. The New Testament assumes that Christ's ordinary world was heaven (Phil.2:6 strongly implies this), where he also received his call, so to speak, to come as Redeemer.[6] There is also no very obvious Refusal of the Call. The closest we get to that is his dialogue with the Father in Gethsemane, which doesn't happen until we are almost at the climactic moment of the whole story. Other elements, however, are very pronounced. What is normally termed the "Tests, Allies, Enemies" stage occupies virtually the whole of Christ's earthly ministry from the calling of his first disciples to the Approach, which starts with the Triumphal Entry into Jerusalem and finishes with his arrest.

This very long Tests, Allies, Enemies section underlines a point that I will make when we get there, which is that this long test is entirely true to life. Relatively few fictitious stories alight here for quite so long—the writers don't want their readers or viewers to lose interest. Exceptions would be those stories that are clearly framed around the idea of an odyssey or quest, such as *The Wizard of Oz* and *Finding Nemo*. In these stories the oversized Tests, Allies, Enemies section is made interesting by all the weird and wonderful personalities that are encountered along the way. In real life, the road is every bit as long as Dorothy's but the characters we meet might not be quite so thrilling or amusing. Great reserves of patience are needed before eventually there is a change of scene: we finally come to the edge of something great. For this reason, I have chosen to call that chapter The Long Road.

And, perhaps, herein lies my main concern. Sure, I am concerned that readers would not miss their calling, and I am concerned that they would not fail to share the elixir once it is all over, Most of all, though, I want to help you see that this long period of testing you are going through had a beginning which was filled with promise, and that it has an appointed end which will overflow with blessing.

---

6. In the Reformed tradition this is described as the Covenant of Redemption, more of a pact between Father and Son than a call as such: Berkhof, *Systematic Theology*, 265–271.

## Discussion:

1. What are the most striking changes that you have noticed in Western culture during your life time?

2. What would you say has been the most decisive moment of your life?

3. Where would you say your life is going at the moment?

# Act 1

# 1:1. The Ordinary World

AT THE START OF any great adventure story there is the "once upon a time. . ." part. This is where everyday life for the hero-to-be is portrayed. It is invariably humdrum. We are given the impression that this day could be any day in the hero's life. Clark Kent is filing, Neo is working on a computer in a cubicle in a large impersonal office, Alice is sitting beside her sister on a river bank feeling bored, Indiana Jones is lecturing a class of inattentive archaeology students. In the Bible we find Joseph wandering the fields looking for his brothers, or David looking after a few of his father's sheep.

The difference, of course, between their ordinariness and our ordinariness, our dead-end job that we've been in for twelve years, our unexciting little block of suburbia where we live, our lack of any exceptional talents, is that we already know that the banality of *their* lives is temporary. In fact, so sure are we that this is the case that, in many ways, those first few minutes of a film are the most exciting part. Those are the minutes that make us stuff our mouths with popcorn in sheer anticipation. The film hasn't had the chance to fail to thrill us yet. The tension is building with every scene because we know something is about to happen and we are taking note of all the ordinary things that we know the director wants us to take special note of because these will be referred back to later on in the plot.

The hero's pre-call life is full of clues about his or her adventure life. All the ordinary things that make up the "once upon a time" of the hero will later be transfigured into the ingredients of high adventure. Every day's filming costs thousands of dollars so nothing will be wasted. Nothing will be left in its original banal condition.

Not only on-screen heroes, but real life heroes seem often to suffer from very inauspicious beginnings. Isaac Newton was a sickly infant and did not, to begin with, excel academically in his schooling. Abraham Lincoln was brought up in a log cabin in grinding poverty, and, in his own estimation as he looked in the mirror at his out-of-proportion arms and legs, wrinkly skin and ears that seemed to "flap in the wind," he was "the ugliest man in the world."[1] He suffered persistent rejection and failure in his political career before gaining, in 1860, the position in which he would become the most celebrated president in American history.

Some people begin in obscurity and are destined to remain there and yet have cast a long shadow across history anonymously. Such a character was New York pastor Jeremiah Lanphier. Born in New York, Lanphier was converted there in Charles Finney's Broadway Tabernacle in 1842. A former businessman, at age 49 he was asked by the trustees of Old Dutch North Church to conduct a visitation program in a last ditch effort to get the dying church back on its feet. There was little success but he was a man of prayer. His prayer to God was a simple question: "What wilt Thou have me

1. Davis, "Abraham Lincoln: Savior of a Nation," 14.

to do?"[2] After getting permission from the church, he distributed some leaflets inviting "merchants, mechanics, clerks, strangers and businessmen" to a lunchtime prayer meeting, he opened the doors to the first meeting on 23 September 1857 at noon:

> Five minutes went by; twenty minutes; twenty-five; thirty—and then at 12.30pm he heard a step on the stairs and the first person joined him. A few moments later there was another, and another, until they numbered six and the prayer meeting began. On the following Wednesday the six had increased to twenty; on the third week there were forty intercessors. . .[3]

The same week news came of a revival that was happening under Phoebe Palmer in Canada. Then, on 14 October came the Bank Panic—a massive financial crash involving 18 leading New York banks suspending operations and the subsequent failure of 5,000 American businesses over the coming year. The onset of the financial crisis had a remarkable affect:

> The prayer meeting grew to one hundred, then others began to start prayer meetings; at last there was scarcely a street in New York that was without a prayer meeting. Merchants found time in the middle of the day to pray. The prayer meetings became daily ones, lasting for about an hour.[4]

By early 1858, Lanphier's original Fulton Street prayer meeting was happening on all three floors of the building. By March of the same year, an entire theater was commandeered for the same purpose. This was packed with 3,000 businessmen who came, not only to pray, but also to listen to a powerful preacher: Henry Beecher. Soon, the newspapers were reporting estimates of 6,000 people across New York attending prayer meetings every day. Soon, most of America's other big cities followed suit: Boston, Chicago,

---

2. Bendroth, "What Wilt Thou Have Me To Do?" 336.

3. Edwin Orr, cited in Whitaker, *Great Revivals*, 76.

4. Ibid., 76–77

Washington (where there were 5 meetings a day: 6.30am, 10.00am, noon, 5.00pm & 7.00pm), Buffalo, Newark, and Philadelphia.

Soon, people began to be converted. By May 1858 there had been some 50,000 conversions in New York (the total population was 800,000). In New England the newspapers were claiming that there were some New England towns where not one person had been left unconverted.[5] By the winter, there were reports of the ice on the Mohawk River being broken so that baptisms could take place there.

In short, one pastor who is as little known today as he was then, was instrumental in transforming the spiritual state of a whole country. Not only that but news of the Prayer Meeting Revival reached Ulster leading to the 1859 Ulster Revival, which was begun by an even more obscure person: a young man by the name of James McQuilkin and his three friends who also started prayer meetings. Once fully underway, this revival became known for the frequent occurrences of people prostrating themselves, sometimes even kneeling down in the mud. On one occasion an entire school full of children was affected in this way, with no human influence at all. As the revival spread, and included Dublin as well as the six northern counties, both Protestant and Catholic alike were affected and there was a dramatic thawing of relations between them. Before long a whiskey distillery in Belfast had to be auctioned, and pubs were forced to close for lack of custom. In October 1859, the Maze racecourse only attracted 500 people instead of the expected 10,000. Judges throughout Ulster had no cases to try, there were frequently no prisoners in police custody and not one crime reported.[6] But who has ever heard of James McQuilkin?

Journalist Deborah Meroff tells of the remarkable missionary couple Pam and Dave Lovett who went on to set up the very first NGO in war-torn Tajikistan in the 1980s called the Central Asia Development Agency. Pam, in particular, had left a nice life behind in Wisconsin where she had been a medal-winning horse rider. This perhaps is a hero story in reverse: auspicious beginnings

5. Ibid., 79.
6. Ibid., 84–91.

sacrificed for a life of dire hardship in a war zone but with colossal impact. Pam and Dave saved the lives of countless people desperate for food and medicine.[7] By the time of the war against the Taliban in the wake of 9/11, their organization was ready to help the fleeing Afghans who were arriving on the Tajik border.

Dietrich Bonhoeffer, is also a hero that turns the Hero's Journey motif on its head at this point. In 1939 he was enjoying a dream job at Union Theological Seminary in New York, having escaped Nazi Germany. Soon, however, there was a growing conviction that he must return to Germany and suffer with his people, a decision, as we will see later, that would cost him his life.

What I want to tell you is that your ordinariness, like the ordinariness of big screen heroes in the opening scenes of a movie, is temporary, but so too might your nice life be. And your transformation into something extraordinary may or may not result in you achieving renown. The only thing that is guaranteed about being a real life hero on a real life hero's journey is that your life will become more and more infused with an ever-clarifying sense of purpose. By the time you get to the middle of your adventure energy might be in short supply, courage might totter, companions might prove unreliable, even the final goal might become blurred in the haze of battle, but there is one thing you will never say. You will never complain that your life has no meaning.

## Discussion

1. Have you an untapped potential, and are the routines of your comfortable life presenting you with no opportunity of exploring it?

2. What *might* God have already said to you about this?

---

7. Meroff, *True Grit*, 58–72.

# 1:2. The Call to Adventure

The familiar life horizon has been outgrown; the old concepts, ideals, and emotional patterns no longer fit; the time for the passing of the threshold is at hand.[1]

1. Campbell, *Hero with a Thousand Faces*, 51.

## The Quietness of the Call

IT'S ALL ABOUT RECOGNIZING the call, a call that often comes to us in hushed tones or in the most ignominious of circumstances, and via the most unlikely of messengers. Have you had the call? For Neo it was a puzzling message on his computer—had any unusual emails lately? For Joseph it was ending up thrown into the bottom of a pit. Through these things the divine breaks through the thin film of surface tension separating us from eternity. He comes and journeys with us in disguise. The incarnation of God into a poor Middle Eastern family was not the only time God has tested us with ordinariness, with the things despised, the things of no account. Your call will not come to you any other way. Sure, some speaker might pick you out of the audience and tell you of your future greatness but the only test of whether what he says is true is, Did the Hidden God already tell me that?

John Kirkby was at a Christian leaders' conference in Sussex. He was queuing for breakfast and soon found himself sat next to a man he had never met before. He shared with the man all that had been in his heart about starting a Christian building society or bank. The man told John Kirkby to ring Nigel. Nigel, apparently, was a venture capitalist and might be able to help. On 6 June 1996, John Kirkby made the phone call that would prove to be the most significant phone call of his entire life. The man, so it turned out, was neither a venture capitalist nor able to help with John's plans. Nigel simply said, "Why don't you see what you can do without needing anyone to help you start or any huge sum of money. What could you do on your own now?"

John relates the rest, "I went straight to my computer. . .I just typed debt counselling. That was it! I knew this was it. . .I had found something I was qualified and able do."[2]

Today, Christians Against Poverty helps over 6,000 people every year to become debt free and is becoming one of the world's leading non-profit debt relief agencies. But the beginning was very

2. Kirkby, *Nevertheless*, 30.

ordinary. It isn't even as though Nigel said anything profound or deep. It was simply the trigger that John Kirkby needed.

For Mother Teresa, all it took was a single phrase from a Jesuit priest on furlough from India: "Each person, in life, has to follow his own road."[3] This one aphorism sparked in her mind the thought that she too could become a missionary and take a road that will lead far from all that had been so familiar and comfortable in her native Skopje.

St Francis (1181–1226), in obedience (or so he thought) to God's call to "rebuild my church," was busy repairing, in a literal sense, ruined chapels, when he came across a leper. He had, for some time felt great compassion for the poor and at this moment, felt a powerful urge to dismount from his horse and go to embrace the poor disfigured leper, so despised and alone. At that moment, the leper vanished out of sight. This became one of a number of decisive moments in the formation of St Francis' call to rebuild the church in a spiritual sense, spurning possessions to reach the poor and the untouchable of society. St Francis believed that the anonymous leper had been an appearance of Christ in disguise.

On 24 May 1738, a rather stuffy, punctilious Oxford don known as Jacky to his family and friends had gone "very unwillingly" to a meeting for Christians of a fairly "enthusiastic" kind that he felt at once drawn to and repulsed by. They were mostly immigrants. The meeting took place in the home of one of these immigrants in a fairly insignificant part of London. He hadn't long arrived when somebody took a book written by Martin Luther about Paul's letter to the Romans. The man started reading artlessly, not from the main body of the text, but from the Preface. "Oh no," Jacky must have thought, "What a bore. He's probably going to read the index as well. I knew I shouldn't have come." Instead of "enthusiasm" being the main danger, sheer dullness was now becoming the major threat. To Jacky's great surprise, something unexpected happened. I will let him tell the rest. . .

---

3. González-Balado, *Always the Poor*, 16.

> About a quarter before nine, while he was describing the change which God works in the heart through faith in Christ, I felt my heart strangely warmed. I felt I did trust Christ, Christ alone for salvation; and an assurance was given to me that he had taken away my sins, even mine, and saved me from the law of sin and death.[4]

That man, as any Methodist will know, was John Wesley. Nothing could have prepared him for the amazing transformation of the British people that he was now going to be an agent of over the coming decades.

In all these moments, the extraordinary breaks into the ordinary. Film trailers often like to draw attention to this: "It was just like any other ordinary day. . ." says the deep, Don LaFontaine-esque voice, as tiny snippets of the hero's pre-adventure life flash in front of us, "when suddenly. . ." Just enough ordinariness is portrayed for us to be able to switch off our incredulity when the extraordinary starts happening. And we need to do the same in real life. Be prepared for a moment in which the impossible is wrested from the teeth of the merely possible.

Jesus, as his custom was, stood up in the synagogue in Nazareth to read. It was just like any other ordinary day of observing the religious customs that he had been brought up with. He read from Isaiah. As soon as he opened his mouth people could sense something different: a freshness, an arresting authority, as though every word was him and he was every word. Then came the moment: "Today, this scripture is fulfilled in your hearing." A religious ceremony that included a reading from a religious text was, all of a sudden, transformed into a "today" moment. "Right now, today," Jesus said, "the Messiah that Isaiah spoke of is among you." Indifference, normally so easy in a religious setting, became impossible now. Within minutes, the whole congregation tried to throw him off a cliff. Things could never be the same again. In this case, a whole congregation was receiving—and refusing—a call.

---

4. Pollock, *John Wesley*, 92.

# ACT 1

## The Inciting Incident

The call, as you may have already noticed, does not always come in the shape of something positive. Paul Scanlon, the pastor of Abundant Life church in Bradford, once said, "without a complaint your vision will perish." This is especially true for those who have received a call from God through witnessing some terrible need or inexcusable injustice. Your response is, "I cannot and will not sit back and let this kind of thing carry on!" It is a complaint that quietly rages within you and keeps you focused on providing that answer even against overwhelming odds.

Elizabeth Fry has now become the face on the back of the Bank of England's Five Pound Note. Known as the "angel of prisons," her first visit to Newgate Prison in February 1813 would change her life forever. Philanthropist Stephen Grellet had visited the men's section and was badly shaken by the squalor he had witnessed but still worse had been the glimpse afforded him of the conditions under which the three hundred women lived, together with their children and new born babies, in two cells and two wards for the mothers with babies. Elizabeth Fry lived not far away and was urged to pay a visit. She did so with a friend, Anna Buxton, and some baby clothes. The smell as she approached the cells was the first thing to hit her: she and Anna began to wretch as the stench of urine, stale sweat, blood, excrement, vomit, alcohol and rotting food assaulted them in the lamp-lit corridor. Next was the growing noise as they approached of crying, wailing, laughing and shouting. Worst of all was the sight of half-naked women who stared into Elizabeth's face with hopeless eyes and with lice crawling in their eye-brows, hair and clothes. She went upstairs to the wards and clothed and cuddled the freezing cold babies and spoke comfortingly to their mothers. Back down in the cell, she and Anna, both devout Quakers, knelt down on the filthy straw. Some of the women knelt around them. Tears flowed as she began to commit the lives of these poor women and their ragged children to God's care, probably the first time anyone had ever bothered to pray for them. Thus began her great life's work. Through trials of her own she worked relentlessly to improve the conditions in Britain's prisons.[5]

Take William Wilberforce. His progress from fashionable parliamentary socialite to slave trade abolitionist was, at first, a gradual one. Steadily, he had, through meeting key people, renewed his boyhood faith in Christ and latterly had become more and more apprised of the true horrors of the slave trade. Then, one night, something happened. While sitting and reading and filling his mind with information about the slave trade, he suddenly saw the gravity of the situation. Somehow, none of the statistical information had moved his heart until he happened upon the death rate among African slaves while en route to the West Indies. "From that moment," recalled Wilberforce, "so enormous, so dreadful, so irremediable did its wickedness appear, that my own mind was completely made up for Abolition. Let the consequences be what they would, I from this time determined that I would never rest until I had effected its Abolition."[6]

Have you ears to hear, have you eyes to see, have you a heart ready and willing to feel and know the call of God to your life's work? Read any statistics lately? Is there something you hate?

The town of Wittenberg was being descended on by hundreds of devout people for the feast of All Saints. All Saints was a mass, due to be held the following day, in which particular stress would be laid on praying for the departed. The year was 1517. Tetzel was an experienced vendor of Indulgences. These were written papal pardons issued in exchange for money. Tetzel entered a neighboring town in solemn procession and began his sermon:

> Listen to the voices of your dear dead relatives and friends, beseeching you and saying, 'Pity us, pity us. We are in dire torment from which you can redeem us for a pittance. . .' Hear the father saying to his son, the mother to her daughter, 'We bore you, nourished you, brought

5. The visit to Newgate is vividly told in: Hatton, *Betsy*, 160–163.

6. Pollock, *Fistful of Heroes*, 31. Altogether, so many died while waiting to disembark, while on board ship, and then while in their first year of work on the plantations that the total death rate was around 50%.

you up, left you our fortunes, and you are so cruel and hard that now you are not willing for so little so set us free. . .' Remember that you are able to release them, for

'As soon as the coin in the coffer rings,

The soul from purgatory springs.'[7]

The truth, as the monk and lecturer Martin Luther knew full well, was that half the money was going straight into Albert of Brandenburg's pockets to help pay off the debts he had accumulated through paying for the position of Bishop. The pope, in order to reimburse himself, issued a Bull of Indulgence with the intention that the other half of the money collected would go on the rebuilding of St Peter's Basilica.

This kind of corruption was already well known to Luther and was an unbearable stench in his nostrils. The arrival of Tetzel and news of the ridiculous sermon he had preached to rouse the faithful, was the last straw. Luther only followed the normal procedure for opening a university debate: he nailed his *Ninety-Five Theses* to the door of the Castle Church of Wittenberg. Yet, the timing turned out to be crucial. A hundred years earlier and he might have been burned at the stake. Now, the people were ready, and the people were flocking to Wittenberg for All Saints Day. Luther couldn't have known at the time that he was helping to usher in a new epoch, that, flawed and sinful though he was, he would be a midwife at the birth of the modern era.

It is the profoundest of mysteries that God can put in your heart a very strong objection to something that is so heartfelt that you are unable to speak of it without bursting into tears. Yet, confront me with the very same injustice and, while I see the wrongness of it, the tears do not flow. I haven't got the call. You have. What will you do with it?

"My food," said Jesus, "is to do the will of Him who sent me and to finish His work" (John 4:34). It is only in doing what we were sent to do that there is food for our souls. Until we find it, we will be forever trying to fill that hunger with other things. Find your food.

7. Bainton, *Here I Stand*, 59–60.

## Discussion:

1. Is there something good that you love doing so much that you forget the clock?

2. Is there something, not related to your personal comfort, that you feel so strongly about that you can't talk about it without feeling like you want to cry?

3. What ordinary incidents have you experienced that have led to an extraordinary outcome?

4. Have you a story of some upsetting event that led to other events that were to be of great benefit to other people?

# 1:3. The Reluctant Warrior

## When God Has His Way

THE BIBLE IS LITTERED with them: Moses, Gideon, Jeremiah, Isaiah. They are people with greatness in them but who can't see it. Gideon does not recognize the divine portrait of him: "mighty man of valor." The reluctance of Moses goes far beyond modesty—he is insistent that he is absolutely not the man for the job. The refusal of the call takes place at the point where there is a jarring dissonance between heaven and earth, a clash of perspectives, a collision of narratives. Trouble is, there is one party to the argument that won't back down. God has never been known to agree to disagree. He is not interested in managing such conflicts towards a mutually agreeable outcome. Or is he?

Perhaps the most celebrated biblical instance of a reluctant recipient of a heavenly summons is Moses. He stands out because he objects to God calling him, not with a single voicing of self-doubt (as in Jeremiah, for instance), but in a succession of five increasingly strident objections. The ludicrous act of trying five times to refuse God is so striking that many Old Testament scholars have put this multiple objection down to the existence of a number of different source documents that are here rather clumsily sewn together resulting in needless repetition. But this negotiation with God is, of course, something that proves entirely characteristic of Moses later on. In Exodus 33–34, Moses is seen bargaining with God in four successive waves, each one succeeding in some way until God, who at the start of the bargaining was ready to destroy Israel and start all over again with Moses, promises first to relent, then to send an angel, then his own presence, and finally to reveal more about this "I AM" name that he gave at the burning bush. It is as though, on that later occasion, Moses wins. But here, on this first encounter with, God must triumph over Moses. Even here, however, there are some gains for Moses:

Moses says, "Who am I to be doing this?" God says, "I will be with you."

Moses says, "What will I say when they say 'who sent you?'" Moses says, "Say I AM has sent you."

Moses says, "But supposing they don't believe me?" God says, "I will give you these signs."

Moses says, "But I'm slow of speech (literally 'heavy of mouth'), God says, "I will be with your mouth."

ACT 1

Moses says, "Nope. Send someone else." Angry, God says, "I am sending Aaron to be your spokesman."

Moses walks away from the encounter with the promise of God's presence to be with him and help him speak, with the beginnings of a revelation of the name and nature God, the ability to work miraculous signs and the assistance of his brother Aaron. Reluctant he may be, timid he is not. The shoulders of God, it seems, are broad enough for honest doubts and objections, even if these are strident and insistent.

History is a tale of human reluctance to answer God's call, and God's determination to draw out the right answer from us. The story of many a great saint follows this pattern, perhaps none more so than in the case of Italian born St Bonaventure (1221–1274). At heart he was the simple Franciscan friar who wanted nothing more than a life of simple devotion. The Vatican had other ideas— and so, perhaps, had God. He rose to become a colleague of the great St Thomas Aquinas, Minister General of his order, spiritual director for the king's sister, and, at the age of 44, was elected to the position of Archbishop of York. This last position was too great an honor for him to accept. Butler's *Lives of the Saints* informs us of the tears with which he begged to be released from such a dignity, and was duly allowed to resign a year later. Having escaped this appointment, he was then offered the position of Cardinal by Pope Gregory X, at which point he ran away. He was then summoned to Rome but stopped at a Franciscan convent in Florence along the way. Two messengers from the Pope found him there doing the washing up. They presented him with the Cardinal's hat. He looked at it with dread. His response was, (something like), "Can you just hang it on that bush over there until I've finished all my duties. Thanks." With great sadness, he eventually donned the hat and came to Rome to become the Pope's right hand man. His first achievement was at the Council of Lyon where he was instrumental in bringing about a union, albeit temporary, between the Eastern Orthodox Church and the Roman Catholic Church. Sadly he died before the Council was over.

If harnessed in the right way, this natural reluctance that most of us feel when sensing the call can be an important time of counting the cost. We feel that the call is to be something greater than seems possible, or nobler than seems fitting. We cannot bear it. Yet if this agony is faced, and we surrender our will to God's, power will come.

It was about 2am and some Passover pilgrims were already making their way to the magnificent temple, not wanting to miss a moment of the awe and celebration that filled the atmosphere. But just across the valley, surrounded by olive trees and bent over a rock was a man sweating blood.[1] He was about to face his greatest trial of strength and prayed, "Father, if possible, let this cup pass from me, nevertheless, not my will but yours be done." Every moment spent at the threshold of an ordeal is a moment spent in Gethsemane. The encounter, if it is to conclude well, must finish with, "Your will be done."

Courage will always be the main character trait needed when pondering a call from God. R.A. Torrey (1856–1928) was the Billy Graham of his day yet, in his early days, he struggled with a terrible fear of public speaking even long after being ordained and in spite of a clear call from God to preach. Every time he was due to speak, he would cling to something, such as the back of a chair, just to prop himself up as sweat poured down his face and his voice warbled its way through his message: "It was agony to preach," he said, and he felt nothing but relief each Sunday night when his preaching duties were over for another week. The breakthrough came the day he realized that it was not in fact him that was being asked to preach, but rather that he was being asked to allow God to speak through him.[2]

Billy Graham himself describes a night on a moonlit golf course where he finally gave in to God. He had struggled with the thought of being only a preacher for the rest of his life. Did he really want to just do this one thing for the rest of his life? "Then I prostrated myself on the dewy turf. "'O God,' I sobbed, 'if you want

1. Inspired by Jim Bishop, *The Day Christ Died*, 200.
2. Pollock, *Fistful of Heroes*, 100.

me to serve you, I will."[3] The invitations to speak did not exactly come rolling in straight away, and he was still a student at the time, but soon enough that process by which one speaking engagement leads to another and reputation spreads propelled him onto the world stage.

Dietrich Bonhoeffer, the famous modern martyr, must have needed courage the day, having fled the Nazis to America, he knew he had to go back to Germany. However, his fear does not show. He is an example of a seemingly unhesitating hero, pausing only to pray and seek the will of God in the garden of the home of the Principal of Union Theological Seminary in New York where he lectured. Having taken sides against the Nazis right from the start and thrown himself into the efforts of Christians in Germany to resist Nazism, he now found himself in New York and safe yet feeling that it was the wrong place to be. On the very eve of the outbreak of war, he concludes:

> I must live through this difficult period of our national history with the Christian people of Germany. I shall have no right to participate in the reconstruction of Christian life in Germany after the war if I do not share the trials of this time with my people.[4]

And so he crosses the threshold of an adventure that would see him involved in a plot against Hitler's life, fall in love and get engaged, get imprisoned and write some of his most thought-provoking work and finally face execution in a concentration camp just weeks before it was liberated by American soldiers.

## When the Refusal Sticks

Campbell makes it clear that there are times when destiny allows the hero's refusal of the call to hold, at least for a while. A common reason for such determined refusal is the memory of past experiences: "Heroes claim to be veterans of past adventures which have

3. Graham, *Just as I Am*, 53.
4. Tinsley (ed), *Dietrich Bonhoeffer*, 39.

taught them the folly of such escapades."[5] What normally happens in such cases is that life's pleasures lose their joy, enthusiasm fades away, vision and purpose disappear and the most terrible and stultifying boredom begins to set in: "Refusal of the summons converts the adventure into its negative. Walled in boredom, hard work, or 'culture,' the subject loses the power of significant affirmative action and becomes a victim to be saved."[6]

This is when we start to accumulate stuff, work on neverending home improvements and perhaps erect a monument or two. This is the moment when Terah took Abraham and Lot and intended to go to Canaan but settled half way and died there. The mantle then fell to his son Abraham to go all the way and become, in Canaan, the father of a new nation.

Even as we try, with all our courage, to respond to the call, our ordinary comfortable world will try to cling to us, try to get us to settle half way: "When you are getting ready to undertake a great adventure, the Ordinary World knows somehow and clings to you. It sings its sweetest, most insistent song."[7] Ever decided that it was right to get out of your job only to find that everybody turns nice all of a sudden? Words of appreciation—or even offers of promotion—that you had longed for, now flow freely. How could they know? They didn't. Wisdom is needed here: perhaps such things are God telling you to stay, or maybe it is just the Ordinary World trying to keep you from your adventure. Perhaps your resolve is being tested.

The Brothers Grimm tell the tale of the wild man, Iron John, that lay at the bottom of a pond in a forest from whence he would reach out a hand and take people and animals down to their watery deaths. He is a hairy, rusty-colored wild man uncovered only by bucketing out the water that was in the pond. Iron John is captured, taken to the palace and locked in a cage. One day, a boy is playing with his golden ball. It rolls into the wild man's cage. The boy, who is only eight, fearfully asks for the ball back. The wild

---

5. Vogler, *Writer's Journey*, 108.

6. Campbell, *Hero with a Thousand Faces*, 59.

7. Vogler, *Writer's Journey*, 110.

man, perhaps not surprisingly says, "Let me out of my cage and I will give you your golden ball back." Writer Robert Bly[8] draws insights from this story for the modern male, who has been taught only to be soft, receptive and gentle. To wrest back something more primal and more fitted for the times in life that require fierceness or resolve, it is necessary to let the wild man out of his cage, claims Bly. Yet he surmises that many men get into their mid-thirties feeling frustrated and unhappy having, once in a while, gone back to the wild man within their souls to ask for the lost ball back.[9] The wild man says, "But first you must let me out of my cage."

The lost ball image is similar to the lost ball in the story of the Frog Princess. There comes a time when we must get it back but it will involve crossing a threshold into something new, releasing unfamiliar energies from their cages. If we don't finally make that step: open that cage or kiss that frog, we will be permanently unhappy. Campbell notes that "'introversion,'"[10] is usually the solution at this point in the monomyth. A time spent taking a journey within resolves the inner conflict that has made us fight off the call, and he assures us, "Not all who hesitate are lost."[11]

## Discussion:

1. Is there a past experience of an ill-conceived or misguided adventure that holds you back from responding now to the call? Are you too "wise" to respond?

2. "Courage is fear that has said its prayers," so the saying goes. What is your deepest fear?

3. Do you struggle with the thought that God could call you to greatness? Do you struggle with being conspicuous?

8. Bly, *Iron John: A Book About Men.*
9. Ibid., 10.
10. Campbell, *Hero with a Thousand Faces*, 64.
11. Ibid.

# 1:4. The Meeting with the Mentor

> For those who have not refused the call, the first encoun-
> ter of the hero-journey is with a protective figure...What
> such a figure represents is the benign, protecting power
> of destiny.[1]

FOR 007, THIS WAS Q, for Luke Skywalker it was Obi-Wan Kenobi,
for Neo it was Morpheus. The mentor is classically a wise old man
or woman that equips the hero for the ordeal ahead. This equipping
often involves the giving of gifts, as with Narnia's Father Christmas
giving a life-restoring potion to Lucy, a sword to Peter and a bow
and quiver to Susan. Sometimes the equipping is not physical but

1. Ibid., 69, 71.

consists in a set of clues that seem cryptic at the time but which will make perfect sense in the special world of the adventure. But one thing all mentor figures have in common is the impression they give that they have been this way before. They know the special world of the ensuing adventure and are in a position to be the best guide available. Hence, the mentor also is the voice of destiny for the hero.

Biblically, examples of mentors tend to differ from the kind that we encounter in the movies. Writers of film scripts will seldom write into the plot a highly nurturing and involved kind of mentor because this makes the hero look weak, as though they need mothering. So the encounter tends to be clipped and as short as possible. The meeting is filled with cryptic aphorisms and abstract philosophy. And, of course, when the hero later shows insight into such murky wisdom we invariably admire them all the more. In the Bible, however, we find a complete spectrum of mentors falling into three basic types. At the movie-like end of the scale is the Voice: the giver of a single phrase or pronouncement. In the middle is the Dazzler: the giver of bursts of enthralling inspiration that arouse the hero's deepest passions. At the most involved and committed end of the scale is the Nurturer: the faithful provider of care and instruction until the hero's life starts to bear fruit and display courage. Let's take a look at these.

## The Voice

In the Bible the role that the mentor normally plays in adventure stories is sometimes taken by God himself, such as at the baptism of Christ. There Jesus is equipped with what he will need for entering the wilderness to be tested by the devil, simply this: knowledge of whose Son he is. A single sentence is sufficient: "This is my beloved Son, in whom I am well pleased."

The mentoring voice often comes to a hero that has already received and accepted the call but is in a state of anxiety. It is an equipping voice rather than a directing voice. For John Bunyan it was a Bible verse that jumped out at him finally releasing him from spiritual and mental torments so strong as to almost prevent him ascending the pulpit steps each time he preached. His inner turmoil threatened to extinguish the flame that would one day write one of the most widely read and translated books of all time: the *Pilgrim's Progress*. After years of torment, as he paced up and down in his house, there came to him a verse from Paul's letter to the Romans: ". . .justified freely by his grace. . ." (Rom. 3:24). The slough of despond was replaced with a fountain of joy that set him free of his guilty feelings. "Now," he says, "I was as one awakened out of some troublesome sleep and dream. . ."[2]

The short sharp encounter seems just the thing for a hero that has answered the call and is sure of it but is hindered in some specific way. It is a spiritual leg-up.

## The Dazzler

The archetypal dazzler is Elijah. Elijah seems to be a remote but brilliant figure who dazzles Elisha and shows him what he'll get if he practices. The relationship begins in a way that must have been a surprise to Elisha. He is ploughing with a team of oxen wondering about his life. He hears some feet approaching in the furrow left behind him. No sooner has he looked around when there is Elijah holding his cloak. Elisha stops. The sun is in his eyes and he cannot see well. In a mere moment the mantle of the greatest prophet who had ever lived rests upon his shoulders. Elijah walks on ahead of him. Elisha, stunned for a while says, "Wait. . .Let me go and say a proper farewell to everyone. Then I'll follow."

John Newton, the now world famous writer of *Amazing Grace* was dazzled by the preaching of George Whitefield when he attended one of his huge three-hour services at Moorefields Tabernacle in London in 1755. Later, a stay in Liverpool coincided with a preaching tour of Whitefield's in the area and the chance came to become acquainted. During that one week, Newton took every

2. Bunyan, *Grace Abounding to the Chief of Sinners*, 257.

chance he could to learn from England's greatest preacher: hearing him speak nine times and eating together five times.[3]

Being dazzled by another person's greatness and gifts seems to be essential in giving a hero a vision of the end game that will keep him or her on track through long delays and contradictions.

## The Nurturer

Deborah mentored Barak in a very involved way. Though she is very straight talking, theirs is a pastoral, nurturing relationship. She nurtures him into the warrior he is destined to be. Her encouragement of him had been so pleasant, so soul-nourishing that he had developed what the mentoring experts would say is an unhealthy dependency on her. He wants her to go with him right into battle.

Some of the greatest people have been the most nurtured. Queen Victoria came to the throne at the tender age of eighteen and, until she married Albert, she basked in three years of mentoring that would last as long as five hours a day in which she would learn the ways of politics. This came courtesy of the mild and kind man after whom one of Australia's premier cities was named, the then prime minister, Lord Melbourne. It is a credit to Victoria and her long reign that she sought out and clung so tenaciously to Lord Melbourne's counsel. She even gave him his own apartment in Buckingham Palace for a time.

There is a growing literature about how to *be* a mentor yet the thing we all need to know about, especially if our adventure has got bogged down in the mire of fears and obstacles, is how to *be mentored*; how to seek out the company of someone who has been where we intend to go. Do we need to be dazzled, or nurtured, or will a mere word be enough? Ask and you shall receive.

3. Pollock, *Amazing Grace*, 137.

## The Life of Christ:

His baptism: Matthew 3:13–17; Mark 1:9–11; Luke 3:21–22.

His meetings with the Father: Luke 5:15–16; 6:12–13; 9:28–36; 22:39–46.

## Discussion:

1. Have you ever been mentored by someone, whether formally or informally?

2. What is it that is most likely to inspire and encourage you: a brief but prophetic word, a highly gifted or skilled example of what you want to become, or a kind soul that is willing to invest time and care in your development?

# Act 2

# 2:1. Passing the Threshold

A NEW CHAPTER IN the life of the hero begins now. He is on the border with the "zone of magnified power."[1] She is about to be ushered into the special world of the adventure. The hero is about to embark upon a journey that will change him forever; a journey in which part of her will die but something new will come forth from within.

1. Campbell, *Hero With a Thousand Faces*, 77.

But before heroes can be allowed to enter this world, there is a test for them to pass. There is normally a threshold guardian or gatekeeper, the troll of fairy tales that guards the bridge across. In some cases this obstinate figure may be a well-meaning ally. The hero himself can see that, beyond the veil, is the unknown. There are untold dangers to face yet the hero must commit the forbidden act to progress: they must cross over.

The threshold guardian takes many forms, ranging from the belligerently hostile and terrifyingly powerful to the type whose role in the story merges with that of the mentor: the source of cryptic sayings, puzzles and clues. In the movies, threshold guardians often move from being an enemy into becoming an ally. In fact, the main task for the hero seems to be to make an ally out of the apparent enemy. For Dorothy while she stood being refused access to the Emerald City this was as simple as bursting into tears. The guard then burst into tears himself and let her and her companions through.

Biblically, however, threshold guardians never become allies. We certainly do not see Goliath bursting into tears in response to a few strums of David's lyre. To the contrary, biblical threshold guardians include the stubborn Pharaoh obstructing Moses, the jealous Potiphar throwing Joseph into prison, the uncharitable Og king of Bashan and Sihon king of the Amorites refusing to let Israel pass harmlessly through their land on their way to the Jordan. For David, Saul was the main obstacle to his destiny and the test was whether or not David would overcome this obstacle in the right way. For the Son of David, the threshold was the wilderness and the guardian was the devil himself. The only possible example of a biblical hero who assimilates a threshold guardian rather than defeating it outright, is the apostle Paul. His past, though threatening to standing his way by disqualifying him utterly for the task, becomes the dark that makes the brightness of Paul's message all the brighter. He makes full use of it, describing himself as the Chief of Sinners who found mercy.

Our threshold guardians may be job interview panels, gallery managers, local government officials, examinations, a controlling parent or spouse, a difficult landlord or boss, or a troublesome trait within ourselves. These are all tests to see whether we are worthy to enter the world of the adventure, and in passing these tests we grow as people. Their job as threshold guardians is to create "psychological readiness"[2] for the ordeal that lies ahead.

Yet, these guardians represent a real obstruction: they are not merely feigning hostility for the purposes of the test like some kind of role play. They must be dealt with somehow or no progress will be made. How do we deal with threshold guardians?

Assuming we want to move forward, there are four options:

## Use Force

Force is needed when those standing in your way cannot be won over and submitting to their will would mean rejecting a call. Florence Nightingale had, from the age of 17, experienced some vivid revelations from God about what her life's work would be but, as a girl born into an aristocratic family—her title was Grand Duchy of Tuscany—her parents were not pleased with her choice of nursing as a career. She acquiesced to their firm resistance for a time but the power of her calling was greater. Finally she announced, at the age of 24, that she would become a nurse. Thankfully, the outrage of her mother and sister did not prevent her from going on to earn her place in history as the Lady with the Lamp. In the Crimean war alone, she was instrumental in reducing the death rate among wounded soldiers from 42 per cent to 2 per cent. Her work in nurse training made her nothing less than the pioneer of modern nursing.

## Outwit or find a way around

William Tyndale's biographer describes the "cold ungenerous reception"[3] that Tyndale received when he went to the Bishop of London, Cuthbert Tunstall, in 1523. Tyndale had gone to meet the bishop to ask for his patronage while he undertook, under the bishop's employment, the translation of the New Testament into

2. Ibid., 84.
3. Demaus, *William Tindale*, 48.

English directly from the original Greek. He had looked forward to this interview for a while, knowing that Tunstall was proficient in Greek and Hebrew (a rare thing in those days) and that he, like himself, was acquainted with the works of Erasmus and Luther. In the event, the silent pacing up and down of the bishop and his general attitude made it clear that, to him, Tyndale was a nobody, someone wasting his time. The bishop had much more time for the high born and significant with whom he could negotiate with great tact and skill to preserve the peace. He was dismissive of Tyndale and his plans, a fact that almost broke Tyndale's heart. Moving, and later fleeing, from place to place around Continental Europe, manuscripts under his arms, would now be his lot. But in the course of so unsettled a life, not only an English Bible but his influential *Obedience of the Christian Man* would fly off the printing presses of Germany and Belgium and find their way to England. Today, about 80 per cent of the more literal versions of the English Bible are still the words that Tyndale chose.

## Assimilate

Supposing your threshold guardian is something that arises from within you? Something about you gives rise to the feeling that you are, unless you can dramatically change, unfitted for the task, positively disqualified. Experience has shown you that you cannot simply lop it off, dispose of it: it is part of who you are. Yet neither do you wish to call a truce with it: it is a genuine obstacle. It could be depression, for instance. Many heroes have suffered in this way. Indeed, Lord Byron invented a new genre of hero: the Byronic hero, such as Manfred, whose greatest enemies are not external pitfalls along the way but the tyrannies of their own soul.

In 1774, William Cowper was recovering from a severe bout of depression that had seen him try to drown himself in a river when he gave us some the best loved hymn lyrics ever written:

> God moves in a mysterious way
> His wonders to perform;

He plants His footsteps in the sea
And rides upon the storm.

He goes on:

Ye fearful saints, fresh courage take;
The clouds ye so much dread
Are big with mercy and shall break
In blessings on your head.[4]

Some time ago I had the joy of supervising an exceptionally good MA dissertation about John Wesley's early infatuation with Sophy Hopkey. This love affair, sometimes glossed over or dressed up in the biographies, took place in the American colony of Savannah over 1736–7 and was disastrous for him. Sophy's father disapproved of their marrying and Sophy grew tired of John's endless prevarications and was soon betrothed to someone else. As priest, John then refused to administer communion to Sophy and her new husband, resulting in severe ill feeling on the part of Sophy's father, with the threat of a lawsuit.

Having set out for Savannah on a mission to evangelize the native Indians, he returned to England in disgrace. Throughout his encounters with Sophy he had discovered deep feelings for her that he had never experienced before, and he seemed unable to know what to do with them. My MA student concluded that this discovery within him of an emotional side to his character would later prove decisive in him formulating his very distinctive views of salvation and sanctification. His revival sermons would later be famous for the strong displays of emotion in his audiences. He himself seemed to come to understand that a true conversion and a deep personal sanctification from sin can often involve powerful emotions, and from these he did not entirely recoil, thanks, perhaps, to his discoveries about himself in Savannah.

4. Shepperd, *The Great Hymns and Their Stories*, 101–2.

## Act 2

# Persuade

Persistent persuasion may be needed when the threshold guardian is not some force from within but a more obvious kind of gatekeeper: someone, for instance, that has the power to veto your ordination, to refuse your manuscript, to pass your paper, to pass a law, or to introduce you to someone important.

In 1956, Queen Elizabeth II, on her first visit to Calabar, Nigeria, made a point of including in her itinerary a visit to the grave of a missionary to lay a wreath. This missionary, a short and hot tempered Scot, showed throughout her tireless years in West Africa, the power of persuasion. Profoundly fluent in the native languages, and content to live in poverty far beyond any mission compound, she won the respect of the chiefs. Her hot-blooded contesting of barbaric and murderous customs saved countless lives. It was the custom, for instance, to kill or abandon any twins that were born. It was believed that one of them must be the offspring of a devil. She personally adopted a number of them as well as successfully outlawing the practice. Not surprisingly, there were occasions when her sharp criticisms drew the anger of tribal chiefs, such as when she rigorously defended a young slave man who was to be summarily executed, without proper trial, for allegedly bewitching a very valuable slave girl who had fallen in love with him and had wanted to run away with him. He had refused, fearing the consequences, and she had then hanged herself. As they waved knives and guns at the missionary, she would not flinch but stared straight back at them all, leaving them awestruck. She reported, "God and one is a majority."[5] The young man was spared. The missionary's name was Mary Slessor. By 1891, her influence over the region was so great that the British Empire made her into its first ever woman vice-consul.[6]

Have you an obstacle? It is because you are ready to cross a threshold. Beyond this threshold lies a new thing, an entirely new thing. You are about to enter the zone in which you will seize your calling. Choose your strategy, and go through.

5. Pollock, *Fistful of Heroes* (Rev.Ed), 201.
6. Ibid., 202.

## The Life of Christ:

His temptation in the wilderness: Matthew 4:1–11; Mark 1:12; Luke 4:1–13.

## Discussion:

1. Can you recall any previous thresholds you have crossed? Who or what were the gatekeepers and how did you deal with them?

2. What are you aiming for? Where do you hope your hero's journey will take you?

3. Why do you want so badly to get there?

# 2:2. The Long Road

THIS IS A SIGNIFICANT new stage. The special world of the adventure has now been entered. The conventional world has been left behind and a new world has swallowed the hero. In this new world, the hero will become something that was not possible to become in the ordinary world. Entrance into it has been a "life-centering, life-renewing act."[1] This new world, however, is "curiously fluid,"[2] fraught with dangers and will bring many trials. He or she will need supernatural aid and will have recourse to return many times to the advice received from the mentor. The hero has entered a labyrinth. It is a place of purifying trials.

> Dragons have now to be slain and surprising barriers passed—again, again, and again. Meanwhile there will be a multitude of preliminary victories, unretainable ecstasies, and momentary glimpses of the wonderful land.[3]

In the movies, this is the part where you are conscious that there has been a decisive shift; a palpable change of scene. The environment has changed, and there is a new set of acquaintances, and a new set of rules. To begin with there might be a time of refreshing in the local watering hole where new acquaintances are made. There the hero gets the latest news, gets a feel for who's who, and the general lie of the land, and usually acquires a side-kick. He starts to gather a team one by one, like Jesus calling his disciples, or like Danny Ocean recruiting his rat pack of eleven to raid three Las Vegas casinos.

Above all the hero must, through many potential diversions, "concentrate on the goal."[4] While the stakes have just been raised and the price of mistakes has become higher,[5] the tests to be faced in this first stage of the ordeal are only a preparation for what is up ahead: the climactic battle, the mid-point of the adventure. Most heroes make many mistakes at this first stage: the whole world they have entered is booby-trapped, but they very quickly wise-up.

The dominant quality that will more and more be required is persistence. Without perseverance no hero will make it to the inner-most cave and the climactic struggle which awaits.

In 1834 Charles Goodyear, owner of a hardware shop in New Haven, Connecticut, happened to buy a rubber life jacket made

1. Campbell, *Hero with a Thousand Faces*, 92.
2. Ibid., 97.
3. Ibid., 109.
4. Vogler, *Writer's Journey*, 135.
5. Ibid., 136.

by the Roxbury Rubber Company and noticed that the hose con-
nector was not well made. He made an improved version of it and
showed it to the manager of the Roxbury Rubber Company who
was duly impressed but confessed that the company was in dire
straits due to the fact that their rubber products were being returned in droves. People who had purchased rubber shoes would
put their feet up near the fire only to find their shoes would melt
and give off a foul odor in the process. Anyone caught out in a
blizzard wearing rubber boots found that they would turn as hard
and inflexible as rock. In the Summer-time, any owners of rubber wagon-covers, rubber piano covers or rubber overcoats who
had not thought to stow them away in a refrigerator would soon
find themselves disposing of a sticky oozing smelly mess.[6] The
company was facing ruin. Charles Goodyear saw his opportunity.
Having no capital, he sold all his furniture and moved his family into lodgings while he worked on experiments in vulcanizing
rubber—the process of making it resistant to extremes of heat and
cold. By accident, he discovered that the addition of nitric acid to
the rubber helped to insulate the rubber against extreme tempera-
tures. Then the financial crisis of 1837 hit. His family was all but
destitute, surviving only on the kindness of friends. Added to this
was a general reluctance to buy rubber products because of the
historic failures of the Roxbury company.

Undaunted, and with his wife still right behind him, he took
to the streets wearing a suit entirely made of rubber to advertise
his wares. Doffing his rubber hat, and flexing his rubber shoes, he
would show off his rubber jacket, rubber waistcoat, rubber shirt,
rubber tie and rubber trousers to anyone who passed. Recognition
eventually came and he received a contract to make mail bags for
the postal service. To his horror, these too began to melt in the
heat of the sun. The nitric acid, it seemed, had hardened only the
surface of the rubber. Undaunted, he continued his experiments,
now using Sulphur following a tip from a former employee of the
Roxbury Rubber Company. One day, while he was showing his
product to someone he dropped some onto a red hot stove. He

6. Thayer, *Men Who Win*, 184.

noticed that the rubber that had been vulcanized with Sulphur, once heated, would become no longer susceptible to any degree of heat or cold. He now set about trying to find out exactly what temperature and duration of heat was needed to cure the rubber.

At this point he received an offer of business from a French company for the original product that he had made the mail bags with, the French being as yet unaware that this earlier product had been faulty. With great integrity, and going against the advice of family and friends, he came clean and refused the offer, promising to inform them of the results of his latest experiments. However, this was the severe winter of 1839–40 and he by now had no means of either clothing or feeding his family. His own health was weakened because of some near fatal exposure to toxic chemicals in the course of his experiments. Despite this, he resolved, in the midst of a blizzard and in spite of the urgings of his wife, to walk to the house of an acquaintance who lived some miles away and ask him for help. Thankfully this duly came. Soon he resolved to go to New York to visit some potential investors, however, on the way, he was arrested and thrown in to prison for debt—and this not for the first time. While there he used the time to write to potential partners. On his release, he found a source of funding for his final, and very expensive, experiments in using heat as well as Sulphur to vulcanize rubber. Finally, his product was perfected. His trials were over and the world began to embrace his rubber. Among the hundreds of different uses for it is, of course, the tire, and in 1898, decades after his death in 1860, in honor of his tireless efforts, the Goodyear Tire and Rubber Company was named after him.

Robert the Bruce, of *Braveheart* fame, was recognized by Pope John XXII as the king of an independent Scotland in 1324. However, at an earlier point in his struggle he had found himself hiding in a cave following a battlefield defeat. On the brink of despair he noticed a spider in the corner of the cave. The spider was hanging by a thread of gossamer and kept trying to climb to the top. Over and over again the spider would fall back but did not give up: "Steadily," wrote Eliza Cook in a poem called *King Robert and the Spider*, "steadily, inch by inch, Higher and higher he got, And a bold little run at the very last pinch Put him into his native cot."[7]

Put it another way: "It takes the hammer of persistence to drive the nail of success."[8] The efforts of first-time novelists are legendary in this regard. Only Shakespeare has sold more books than Agatha Christie, yet she faced five years of continual rejection. J.K. Rowling's agent received twelve rejections before Bloomsbury, on the persuasion of the editor's eight year-old daughter, reluctantly acceded to publish. The last four in Rowling's *Harry Potter* series would end up being the fastest selling books in history. With comments like "anthologies don't sell," Jack Canfield and Mark Hansen received 140 rejections of *Chicken Soup for the Soul.* It has sold 125 million copies. Even the well-established C.S. Lewis endured years of rejection when he wanted to branch out into children's fantasy. His *The Chronicles of Narnia* has now been translated into 47 languages. Beatrix Potter did not even succeed in gaining a publishing contract for *The Tales of Peter Rabbit* and resorted to self-publishing it. It has sold 45 Million copies. W.M. Paul Young, in the face of 20 rejections, resolved to do the same for his *The Shack.* It has sold 15 Million. Kenneth Grahame was told that his *The Wind in the Willows* was nothing more than, "An irresponsible holiday story that will never sell." It has sold 25 Million copies. Frank Baum was told that his story about the Wizard of Oz was "Too radical of a departure from traditional juvenile literature." Perhaps the prize for the most outspoken rejection of a novel goes to the editor who wrote: "An endless nightmare. I think the verdict would be 'Oh don't read that horrid book." That horrid book was H.G. Wells' *The War of the Worlds*, a book that has stayed in print ever since it was first published in 1898.[9]

This enormous demand for persistence, which increases steadily with time, is often understated in films for the simple reason

7. http://mynoteslibrary.com/html/english_X_King_Bruce_And_The_Spider.html [accessed 5 April 2016].

8. John and Stibbe, *Box of Delights*, 151.

9. http://www.litrejections.com/best-sellers-initially-rejected/ [accessed 5 April 2016].

that the screen writer does not want the plot to lose momentum and the audience to lose interest. In the movies, this stage is punctuated with exciting and dangerous encounters. The reality is closer to what Campbell originally saw, which is that it is a season of going steadily deeper into a labyrinthine world haunted by an enemy and in which the help of allies becomes crucial. The ordeal stage in any adventure can be grim, and in real life, of course, we do not know for sure that there will be a happy ending. We can only hope.

However, we are not alone. Even if there are no earthly allies we can reach out for, the writer to the Hebrews assures that there will always be the "great cloud of witnesses" that are cheering us on from beyond the grave. No matter how friendless our ordeal may be, we can at least claim their support, so that we "run with endurance the race that is set before us."

So what is the strategy for getting through this first phase of the ordeal? Hebrews 12:1–2 seems to give us these:

1. Draw strength from your allies.

The writer to the Hebrews makes clear that, even if you are enduring your ordeal without a friend in the world, you have a huge host of dead ones: people from beyond the grave who are gathered on tier upon tier of the amphitheater cheering you on. And you can find out all about their lives in the countless biographies and lives of the saints that have been written. If, however, there is someone that you can share your victories and setbacks with and pray with regularly, this will help you through. Every hero needs an ally, even if it is a buffoon of a side-kick. They all have one.

2. Identify your excess baggage.

The Greeks would compete in the nude. The Greek word for this is *gymnos*. Perhaps you can guess the English word that is derived from it. Your opponent knows that there is nothing more effective at getting you to abandon your mission than to weigh you down, to burden you. You will become so weary you will go back to a life of ease and forget all about the dreams you once had.

3. Maintain your position.

When I was in my late twenties I decided it was about time I learned to drive. As anyone will know who has learned to drive later in life like me, it is much harder at that age. My lessons were often very stressful. I would come home after a Saturday morning lesson and, to unwind, I would turn on the TV. Inevitably there was always a black-and-white World War II submarine film on. I had no idea quite so many of these had been made. There was a different one every Saturday morning yet they all had the same basic elements: there were sweaty, anxious faces as one depth charge after another shook the submarine and made the lights flicker, there were torpedoes that narrowly missed the hull, there was always a leak and some guy in a thick woolly jumper who has to get very wet while he turns the stiff wheel of a hatch and eventually shuts out the water. Despite all the dangers that surrounded them, the most frequent instruction was: "maintain position." Apart from the occasional dive, all they needed to do was maintain their course and they would get through their ordeal. It is a race "marked out for you." You have to stay on the track and keep going. You have to hold course.

## The Life of Christ:

His setting his face like flint to complete the final journey to Jerusalem: Luke 9:51; Mark 10:32–34.

## Discussion:

1. What are the human resources around you? Who are the people you can count on?
2. Is there something that you are hanging onto that is weighing you down? What can you jettison? What is it that is sapping your strength?

3. How many rotas, committees and meetings are you committed to? Are you bearing fruit or just busy?

4. As far as you can tell, are you still on course or have you strayed onto bumpy track that is making progress impossible?

# 2:3. The Approach

THIS IS THE STAGE that we experience when we have just been told that the job of our dreams is finally ours. The fulfilment it will bring cannot be denied and we are beside ourselves with excitement, yet we are also aware of the far greater pressures that await. Or, we have been offered a place on a course, or invited to give a keynote address, or awarded a prestigious contract. You get the picture. It is a moment that signals the end of a long struggle but the beginning of challenges you have never faced before.

This episode is probably best explained by the emotions associated with it. There are three:

## A Momentary Sense of Triumph

In the movies you can recognize the change of scene by the fact that there tends, at this point, to be a camp fire moment. There have been many trials but many victories too and the hero takes time to celebrate. The hero and his or her team have finally arrived at base camp. They have completed their journey and are poised for the final assault. This moment affords the viewer or reader a rest from the constant trials and challenges. There is a release of tension and a break from conflict.

However, there is also a growing awareness that the biggest test is still up ahead. In the movies, this combination of rest and trepidation forces the characters to focus on the present, to give each other a moment of quality time since who is to say if it will be their last. If there is going to be a love scene it will be now.

In the Gospels we find Jesus reclining in the home of Mary and Martha, with the restored Lazarus also present. The home is in Bethany, the last stop before Jerusalem, the city that kills the prophets.

In 1974 Chuck Colson, following his conversion the previous year, chose to confess to his involvement in the Watergate scandal. Having done his best to make good a situation that was going to be bad for himself and his family, there came the point when all he could do was wait and hope for leniency on the part of Judge Gesell. In the days before the trial family and friends rallied round yet, for Colson, "the painful suspense mounted."[1] On the day of sentencing, the outcome was worse than anyone had imagined: a jail sentence of one to three years and a fine of $5,000. He had no speech prepared for the throng of reporters waiting for him but found himself saying words that were to define a life that would see

---

1. Colson, *Born Again*, 260.

him decorated with the Templeton Prize for Progress in Religion and the Presidential Citizens Medal: "What happened in court today was the court's will and the Lord's will—I have committed my life to Jesus Christ and I can work for Him in prison as well as out."[2] As founder of the Prison Fellowship and of the Chuck Colson Center for Christian Worldview his work for his Lord proved undeniably fruitful right up until his death in 2012 at the age of 80.

## Excitement and Anticipation

As the hero looks to the next step there is a re-visioning, a realignment towards the goal. In an action movie this is when the final assault is planned and each team member is assigned their role. In *The Lion, The Witch and the Wardrobe* news of Aslan's death infuses Peter with a clarified sense of calling and duty, and Aslan's army of creatures now looks to him for orders and a battle plan.

As heroes look to the next step, this is where the gift of prophecy comes into its own. Paul is warned by the prophet Agabus that when he enters Jerusalem with the monetary gift from the Gentile churches, he will be bound and arrested.

The Hebridean revival of 1949–52 was a spectacular religious awakening which swept across the islands of the Outer Hebrides. Its most famous event took place in a little granite house, which can still be seen today. This house physically shook at the close of an impassioned prayer meeting.

This revival was preceded by and then directed by an unusual amount of prophetic activity. Peggy Smith, an 84 year old blind lady and her sister Christine, an arthritis sufferer had been praying relentlessly in their tiny cottage for a revival to come. One night Peggy saw in a dream the church full of young people and felt a clear promise from God that He would '. . .pour water upon him that is thirsty and floods upon the dry ground.' Peggy shared her dreams with the minister James Murray Mackay, whose wife also then had the same dream with the additional detail of a stranger

2. Ibid., 273.

standing in the pulpit whose name was later revealed in a vision to Peggy: "Duncan Campbell."

Mackay called a prayer meeting three nights a week in response. Mackay then sent for evangelist Duncan Campbell who was in the middle of an outreach on Skye and would not be available for another year. The two sisters, undeterred, predicted that Campbell will be with them within two weeks. Miraculously, the convention was cancelled and Campbell traveled to Lewis. No sooner had Campbell arrived when a deacon was taken over by a strong prophetic anticipation and said to him, "Mr Campbell, God is hovering over. He is going to break through."

The first meeting produced no remarkable results until about 30 of the people there, including Campbell, decided to spend the night in prayer after the service. They went to a nearby cottage. Campbell himself relates what happened:

> God was beginning to move, the heavens were opening, we were there on our faces before God. Three o'clock in the morning came, and God swept in. About a dozen men and women lay prostrate on the floor, speechless. Something had happened; we knew that the forces of darkness were being driven back, and men were going to be delivered. We left the cottage at 3am to discover men and women seeking God. I walked along a country road, and found three men on their faces, crying to God for mercy. There was a light in every home, no-one seemed to think of sleep.[3]

By the time daylight came a stream of buses had arrived at the church from every part of the island, yet no-one could find out who told them to come. The converts multiplied. Prayer meetings routinely carried on until the early hours of the morning. At 4am one morning, after the close of a prayer meeting, Campbell was called to a local police station where he found people gathered from the other end of the parish, some lying on the road, others beside a cottage, others behind a peat stack, all crying to God for mercy.

---

3. Cited in Whittaker, *Great Revivals*, 114.

The directions from blind Peggy continued to flow. She told
Campbell to visit an area that had been resistant to the revival.
Campbell was reluctant and did not feel that God was calling him
there. Peggy prayed with him:

> Lord, You remember what you told me this morning,
> that in this village You are going to save seven men who
> will become pillars in the church. Lord, I have given Your
> message to Mr Campbell and it seems he is not prepared
> to receive it. Oh Lord, give him wisdom because he badly
> needs it!

A decade earlier in Haarlem, Holland, Corrie Ten Boom's father becomes prophetic too, but this is with grave foreboding. The
year was 1940 and the Prime Minister of Holland had just given an
announcement that Germany would respect Holland's neutrality
and there would be no war on Dutch soil. Corrie's father abruptly
turned off the radio set: "It is wrong to give people hope when
there is no hope . . . It is wrong to base faith upon wishes. There
will be war. The Germans will attack and we will fall."[4] Within five
hours the invasion of Holland was underway. And so would begin
the Ten Booms' remarkable story of hiding Jews in their home and
of being incarcerated themselves, an ordeal from which neither
Corrie's father nor her sister Betsie would survive. Corrie immor-
talized for us all the dying words of Betsie: "There is no pit so deep
that He is not deeper still."[5]

## A Sense of Foreboding

In missionary biographies the newly arrived missionary has her
first tour of the neighborhood. She is frequently overcome with revulsion or outrage at the conditions people are living in and the in-
dignity with which they treat one another. Jackie Pullinger became
well known in the 1980s for her remarkable successes in Hong
Kong's Walled City where she saw countless addicts freed through

4. Ten Boom, *The Hiding Place*, 62.
5. Ibid., 197.

the power of the Spirit. However, her first few days in Hong Kong in 1966 would have been enough to discourage anyone lacking the calling she had received.

First, she encountered a familiar feature of the Approach stage: a second threshold guardian. At this stage we approach the inmost cave, the special world within the special world, the heart of the adventure. We might need to go through a similar process to when we got past the grumpy old troll and first crossed the threshold. In Jackie's case it looked as though all was lost and she would be sent home by the grumpy immigration officers as soon as she arrived. She had come with only £6, no job and nowhere to live. The immigration officers apparently suspected she was going to earn money through prostitution. Then, she remembered that her mother's Godson was a policeman living in Hong Kong. Knowing a policeman gave her instant credibility and freedom to enter the territory.

Jackie soon received an invitation to visit a nursery school and church in what she thought was going to be a quaint little walled village. Via a narrow gap between shops she found herself admitted into another world, a world of "ramshackle skyscrapers" that were built so close together (at least 30,000 people were living in six acres of land) that almost no light penetrated to the narrow slimy alley ways that she was ushered along by her elderly host. "I will never forget the smell and the darkness, " writes Jackie, "a fetid smell of rotten foodstuffs, excrement, offal and general rubbish." She goes on:

> As we went my guide gave me a running commentary; on my right was a plastic flower factory, on my left an old prostitute who was too old and ugly to get work. So instead she employed several child prostitutes to work for her. . . Next we reached the door to the illegal dog restaurant, where the captured beasts were flayed to death to provide tender dog steaks; then the pornographic film-show house, a crowded lean-to shed.[6]

This is the point at which the hero faces the full enormity of the task ahead, the sheer power of evil. It is an evil that has been left to flourish largely undisturbed for so long that it has established a

---

6. Pullinger & Quicke, *Chasing the Dragon*, 35.

sordid yet sophisticated citadel. In the case of the Walled City, the criminal activity was closely guarded by a network of watchers and whisperers. It was overseen by an extensive hierarchy of evil that could respond rapidly to intruders.

As we think of Jackie Pullinger, Elizabeth Fry, Mary Slessor and countless other examples, it seems that of the very few people that have ever been to the world's darkest places and taken on the evil powers that rule them, it is Christian women that have excelled the most. Time and again we find them describing the putrid smells and the outrageous inhumanities and not stopping there but devoting their lives to the relief of the oppressed.

## Lessons of the Approach

As we reach the Approach stage we face a dual danger. There is the danger that we will not stay there long enough. The camp fire moment of joyful recollection, of celebration is needed. We must mark the occasion and we must rest for long enough to gather the strength we will need for what is to come. But there is also the danger that we will stay there too long. Perhaps the sense of foreboding will be too much for us: the trials we have already been through have tested our courage to breaking point and we cannot go any further.

The best way to avoid both errors is to clarify your vision. What is the goal? Exactly what is the grail that you set out on your quest to obtain? Your idea of what this is may have changed over the course of your quest, and that is fine, normal in fact. But now is the time to foster within your heart the clearest picture yet of what exactly the prize is. You will then be emboldened to go and seize it.

## The Life of Christ:

His last stay in Bethany: Matthew 26:6–13 / Mark 14:3–9 / John 12:2–11

His Triumphal Entry: Matthew 21:1–11 / Mark 11:1–11 / Luke 19:29–44 / John 12:12–19

His Last Supper: Matthew 26:17–29 / Mark 14:12–25 / Luke 22:7–30 / John13–16

The Garden of Gethsemane: Matthew 26:36–46 / Mark 14:32–42 / Luke 22:30–46 / John 18:1

## Discussion

1. Do you feel excited yet apprehensive about some new development in your life?

2. The Approach is a re-visioning, realigning time. How sure are you that you are on course for the right goal?

# 2:4. The Fight

WE ARE NOW COMING to the central defining crisis in the hero's journey: "Everything in the trip has been leading up to this moment, and everything after it will be just going home."[1] This is not to say there will be no more conflict after this. To the contrary, the final denouement is yet to come. The final struggle normally hap-

1. Vogler, *Writer's Journey*, 159.

pens on the way back to the ordinary world towards the end of the story. But what we do have here is the destination of the journey the hero set out on. This is the summit of the mountain they set out to climb, the heart of the labyrinth, the deepest cave. Even the final fight at the end will happen only because of what takes place here.

This central drama is about wresting life from the teeth of death. The stakes have been raised to the highest possible point within the narrative. It is either literally or figuratively a meeting between life and death. The hero will either get what they came for, or die trying. But even if they do not literally die, there will be something about them that is doomed to not survive this encounter.

This moment of death can take three forms, the most desirable first; the least desirable last:

## A Voluntary Self-Sacrifice

Christ is, of course, the supreme example in surrendering himself to arrest and trial, knowing what was to befall him. And he had long insisted that the path of true discipleship must figuratively entail the same thing: a denial of self and a taking up of the cross.

In action movies, the hero certainly volunteers for the fight but tends not to literally die. Instead the hero ends up in such a titanic struggle with the forces of evil that they appear *to the audience* to have died. Vogler describes vividly his feelings when he saw a preview of that brief but agonizing moment in *Star Wars* when it appears as though Luke Skywalker has actually died: "With the hero dead, who was I in this movie?"[2] These films draw the audience into a vicarious and risk-free brush with death, together with the surge of survivor's euphoria that follows. However, normally the hero does not blithely cheat death and emerge unchanged. The experience means that something of the old person, something of their old ego has truly died and a new chastened version of them emerges. Their death and rebirth has been cathartic, and the audience experiences a faint simulation of that catharsis.

2. Ibid., 162.

Real self-sacrifices are, of course, nothing like watching an action movie. In the early sixties, one young woman, by the name of Sally Trench, had been on an ill-defined quest all through her rebellious school life. One night, while on her way back to her parents' very comfortable home in St John's Wood, she found herself face to face with the life she had been casting around for. She sat between two homeless men on a bench in Waterloo Station. This turned into a nightly visit with a flask of coffee and cigarettes, which turned into an ever deepening involvement in the lives of men whom society had rejected and who had themselves rejected society. Winning their trust was slow, and trying to help them back on their feet in life was faltering and heart-breaking. She began more and more to live her life as one of them, even reaching the point of total mental and physical exhaustion helping to run a home for them. After recovering she continued walking miles all over London bringing food and comfort to meths drinkers, teenage drug addicts, prostitutes. Eventually she decided that, to maintain her sanity she would keep a diary of her experiences. In the end this became the best-selling book *Bury Me in My Boots* of 1968,[3] skyrocketing her to a rather unwelcome fame. To read her story is to be overwhelmed by the example of someone with a profound faith in God who pours her life out for those who live and die unloved. A decade later she recollected:

> I've always felt close to God, and I certainly feel close to God now, but in those years among the meths drinkers and down-and-outs, the young beats and drug addicts, there was a special dimension to it all. I've never been so close to God before or since, as I was then. I felt that God's love was flowing through me to those people, and that I was receiving his love for me from them, too.[4]

Auschwitz has, understandably enough, become synonymous with some of the gravest question marks we might put against the life of faith. More than anything else it prompts the question, "Where was God?" It comes as a surprise then to learn of how one man's

3. There is a more recent edition with an epilogue: Trench, *Bury Me in My Boots*. London: Hodder & Stoughton, 1999.

4. Cooper, *Meeting Famous Christians*, 82.

self-transcending love for others came like "a shaft of light in the darkness,"[5] revealing the "deepest essence of humanity."[6] That man was St Maximillian Kolbe, a Polish Catholic priest who was arrested by the Gestapo in Warsaw in 1941 for having circulated subversive literature. Throughout his time at Auschwitz he became known for his total concern for others, often allowing others to rush forward for meagre offerings of bread leaving none for him. He reasoned that his fellow inmates had families to return to one day, while he had no such ties. One day, three prisoners escaped. Whenever there was an escape, all the remaining prisoners were made to pay: ten lives for every one escapee. Their deaths would be slow: shut away in an underground cell without food or water. On this occasion, all the prisoners were kept on parade in the mid-Summer heat for an entire day waiting for the selection to begin. Finally, at 7pm, the Kommandant began picking out his first ten, his assistant brusquely shoving them forward from the line. The ninth man was selected who promptly wailed allowed and cried out: "My wife, my children, I shall never see them again!" Within seconds, an older prisoner with round wire spectacles was stood in front of the Kommandant asking very politely for permission to take the place of the ninth man, explaining simply that he was a Catholic priest. Permission was granted and the man was saved and survived the war, though tragically lost both sons to Russian shells in the closing months of the war.

Kolbe took his place in the underground bunkers with the other prisoners that had been selected to die. He led them all in prayers and singing through the last days of their lives. Nearly two weeks later, Kolbe was the only man still conscious, sat on the floor and leaning against a wall praying under his breath. Three others remained alive but were unconscious. Lethal injections were then administered so as to free up the cells for another batch of prisoners. The effect of Kolbe's death upon the morale of the prisoners above ground was greeted as an "announcement of victory," which had "the force of an electric shock."[7] Wendy Craig explains it best:

5. Craig, *Six Modern Martyrs*, 127.

6. Ibid., 129.

7. Craig, *Six Modern Martyrs*, 129.

They had come perilously near to becoming dehumanised, to seeing themselves through the contemptuous eyes of their SS masters, without value or meaning. And then suddenly one man had revealed the truth that their degradation had hidden from them: that there is one human freedom that can never be taken away, the freedom a man has to choose his inner response to his fate, to soar above his own personal agony, to transcend himself.[8]

Without doubt, the very greatest stories of the lives of the faithful are those that center upon a Christ-like moment of voluntary self-sacrifice. These stories remind us that the whole Christian life is cruciform. Christian discipleship is a brave meeting with death, whether physical or metaphorical. Out of that meeting, life and love win back their thrones and reign again in human hearts that are so easily pulled away by evil's doomed appeals.

## A Setback

Friedrich Handel enjoys a place in history alongside Bach, his contemporary, as truly one of the founders of classical music. However, on 8 April 1741, at the age of 56, after years of struggling with debt and feeling deeply discouraged, he played his farewell concert. For years he had been catering to the London craze for Italian style operas but the fashion for the genre was dying out, and he was facing ruin. Soon, however, an invitation came his way from the Lord Lieutenant of Dublin to write a biblical oratorio. Oratorios were just coming into fashion and had the benefit of not requiring an expensive set and costumes, just choirs of singers who told the story in song. In August 1741, it took Handel a miraculous three weeks to write the entire oratorio, stretching to 260 pages of manuscript.[9] The title was *Messiah*. While writing it he scarcely slept or ate and was consumed with love for the Lord. A friend intruded on him to find him on the floor crying like a baby. He later reported: "Whether I was in the body or out of my body when I wrote it I

8. Ibid., 127.

9. Kavanagh, *Spiritual Lives of Great Composers*, 20.

know not."[10] The effects of the performances of *Messiah* have been still more remarkable. The very first performance of it, just like so many after it, was a benefit concert leading to the release of 142 men who had been imprisoned for their debts.[11] Both its composition and its impact upon generations of people have been unique phenomena in the history of music. To this day, though the piece was originally performed at Easter, sales, downloads and performances of it reach a huge peak every Christmas.[12]

Sheila Cassidy experienced a major setback when she was working in Chile in the early seventies. She was a doctor and went out to Chile initially with a view to broadening her experience and developing her career. She was soon face to face with abject poverty and began to minister to people's hopelessness as well as to their physical need. Then the coup happened and President Allende came to power. Soon, people were disappearing or being imprisoned and tortured. Sheila knew that the decision to stay at this point was momentous. It would eventually mean that she would find herself treating someone who was on the run from the government. She would then be targeted as a revolutionary sympathizer and would be in grave danger. Sure enough, that day came in November 1975. Without hesitation she treated the infected bullet wound of a left wing revolutionary, operating on the man's leg and leaving him in the care of the nuns to whom he had fled. Within days, she was arrested by armed plain clothes police and taken to an interrogation center. There she was tortured with electric shocks and questioned for as much as twelve hours a day. She also spent three full weeks in solitary confinement. Under intense pressure from the British government, she was released eight weeks later and sent home. There she took full advantage of the media interest to speak of the plight of the people of Chile and all the oppressed people of Latin America.

---

10. Pauli, *Handel and the Messiah Story*, 51, cited by Kavanagh, *Spiritual Lives of Great Composers*, 20.

11. Kavanagh, *Spiritual Lives of Great Composers*, 20.

12. Kandell, "The Glorious History of Handel's Messiah," *Smithsonian Magazine*. Online: http://www.smithsonianmag.com/arts-culture/the-glorious-history-of-handels-messiah-148168540/?no-ist [accessed 18 August 2016].

She also spoke of the spiritual experiences she had while in captivity. God came near during her torment and agony, but there was a battle to win in her faith. In her prayers she often found herself asking God to set her free but felt no peace. It felt better to say, "Not my will but Thine be done." Then she found a profound peace, and even joy. She says:

> If we can come to want only what God wants, then we are in a curious way untouchable, for then loss of property, of good name, of health, or even of life hold no fears, for if that is what God wants, then we have peace.[13]

When asked about how she lives her life in the light of her experience in Chile, she explained:

> I try to live life *abandoned* to the will of God in little things and in big things, striving with every fibre of my being to want only what He wants, and to allow Him to be free to do whatever He wants, whether it be successes or failures. This makes it possible for me to be much less vulnerable than I was before, when I cared much more about what people thought and said and my safety.[14]

## A Heart-breaking Loss

Lesley Bilinda, a Scot, was married to a Tutsi man by the name of Charles. She worked for Tear Fund while he pastored a church in Kigali, Rwanda. The country had often undergone periods of unrest and she, like all her neighbours, was well adjusted to the fact that the streets were not safe at night. This was normal. But by early 1994, tensions were mounting. Nevertheless, she went away as planned with her sister on a holiday to Mombasa, Kenya. Charles did not think it safe as a Tutsi to travel given the situation with Hutus seeking out Tutsis so Lesley reluctantly went without him. Within three days she tuned in her radio in Mombasa to hear the BBC World service announce the deaths of the presidents of Rwanda and Burundi,

13. Cooper, *Meeting Famous Christians*, 109.
14. Cooper, *Meeting Famous Christians*, 109–110.

together with the murder of the Rwandan prime minister and of ten Belgian troops.[15] Hutu militia were now on the streets of Kigali murdering people in their thousands. The ethnic cleansing had begun.

Charles' body was never found and for a while Lesley held onto the hope that he might be alive, but through subsequent visits to the devastated country she was able to reconstruct his last days: the compound where he took refuge before he was captured and shot. Many of the people Lesley had known and worked with either had not survived or had been tragically bereaved like her. One million Rwandan lives had been lost, their bodies often left to rot or dumped in the river. Many survivors showed the most astonishing forgiveness and faith.

Back in Edinburgh, Lesley, though severely traumatized and grief-stricken, slowly recovered. She held a memorial service for Charles, and soon set up a fund in his honor aimed at providing higher education training in the UK for Rwandans following the deaths of so many educated and skilled people. She was left with many questions but put some of her thoughts into a semi-poetic form in her diary:

> Lord Jesus, you've been there already;
> You didn't shy away,
> You didn't drift up to heaven.
> But you suffered
> The humility and degradation
> The injustice and disgrace
> The pain, the torment, the torture
> The agony of mind and body.
> You've been there already
> And you know.[16]

---

15. Bilinda, *Colour of Darkness*, 75.
16. Ibid., 223.

## ACT 2

## Lessons of the Fight

For all of us who are on a quest there will be a defining conflict. It may be a conflict with ourselves that is fought and won, just as it was for Sheila Cassidy and her resolve to abandon herself to God's will alone. In fact, every challenge that greets us from outside will entail a conflict within. Maximillian Kolbe seemed to win the fight against his own self-preservation instantly because of his many rehearsals for it by always putting others first when the bread came round.

The fight, then, is always a fight with ourselves but it will take many forms. It could take the form of a voluntary laying down of your life for the sake of God or others. This might actually involve giving up your physical chances of survival, but more commonly it will be the setting aside, for instance, of a cherished career ambition in deference to a vocation that is to the disdain of all but God alone, or it will be a decision for downward mobility in an acquisitive culture that only understands property ladders and investments. The triumph over self might be foisted on us by some setback which forces us to lay hold of God like Handel writing *Messiah* in three weeks. Many who are creative will recall the worst failures, the most withering reviews or the most paltry sales as a game-changing experience. Often it is the masterpiece which follows the flop. Or it may be that we find ourselves mourning the loss of something or someone or the end of something: a way of life, a set of friends, a job. Our suffering opens our eyes to the suffering of Christ on our behalf and tenderizes our heart to the afflictions of others.

All of these are deaths out of which life wishes to spring. Through these we grasp a prize that will prove definitive of all that we will bring to the world from that moment. It is a defining struggle.

## The Life of Christ:

His trial and crucifixion: John 18–19.

## Discussion:

1. Is there something that you know you must lay down for God or others?

2. Do you languish in discouragement because of setbacks or disappointments? Might this be an opportunity for something new to come forth?

3. Are you mourning the loss of something or of someone or of some earlier way of life? What *might* God be saying through this?

# 2:5. The Prize

THE BOY GETS THE girl, the knight seizes the grail, the army raises the flag, the scientist makes the discovery, the thinker sees the truth, the mystic breaks through to peace with God. This is the moment we will love to speak of to any who will listen: the moment your fiancée said "yes," the time you suddenly saw the truth of something, the occasion you first committed your life unreservedly to God, the minute Christ declares, "It is finished!" and expires in triumph.

This is the moment when you realize you got what you came for. It is not until this point that the realization dawns that we have been a battle ground but now our true destiny has won. All the way through the journey we have been aware that we have been increasingly conflicted. The external struggles have merely brought out the internal struggles more clearly. We have struggled on in the tension between the already and the not yet, between the flesh and the Spirit, between self-actualization and self-transcendence. But now, one side has won and we are whole. At long last, what our future is made of has triumphed. The evil forces clawing us back to who we once were have been prized from us and have gone screaming back to hell. We are now one person with a single heart, not a divided will. We have been broken and made whole, died and risen again.

With this seizing of the sword, the whole of Act II, the biggest part of the story, will draw to a close. There are two things to do at this stage.

## Celebrate

"Triumph may be fleeting but for now they savor its pleasures."[1]

It does not seem long since we last celebrated—we did so when we understood that all the preparatory tests were over and we were finally at the very gates of the destination of our quest. And we will have cause to celebrate again when we finally arrive back in the ordinary world with the elixir to share. Conflict has been growing in intensity. Initially, trials were long but mild. Persistence was needed. Now, the tests have been short but intense. Courage has been summoned from the deepest parts of us. But alongside this trend towards greater intensity, reasons and opportunities to celebrate have also been increasing. It is time for another celebratory camp fire moment.

1. Vogler, *Writer's Journey*, 175.

I still vividly remember the intense joy of the days immediately following my conversion. I went to stay with the friend with whom I had spent many an hour talking about faith in the run up to finally committing my whole life to Christ. We had been art students together. The Gloucestershire countryside around the village of Stonehouse where he lodged seemed exceptionally verdant and full of interest. I had been on many long walks across other parts of the Cotswolds all through my troubled adolescence but never experienced this. My friend was a very late sleeper but I was a relatively early riser. Each morning I would sit in a tussocky field in the sunshine overlooking the valley below and feel a joy I had never known before. I would pray and thank God but even when I stopped praying, the joy kept bubbling away inside me. It is with me now.

I soon came across the story of Doreen Irvine, the woman who, in 1965 had gone from being a heroin addict, prostitute, stripper and powerful witch to a devoted follower of Christ. This had been via an ordeal that saw 16 demons cast out of her, every one of which would speak out in protest audibly to her and, via her voice, to the Rev Arthur Neil who was casting them out. Exhausted but free she convalesced in the rural home of Mr. and Mrs. Parker, whom she came to refer to fondly as "Mom" and "Dad." Though my own deliverance from darkness had not been half as harrowing as hers, I could identify instantly with her description of life in the immediate wake of her life-and-death struggle:

> The whole world appeared beautiful. I loved everyone and everything in this great big wonderful world that God had made . . . As I walked through green fields into the thick woods my heart sang. I danced for sheer joy at all I saw, at all that Jesus Christ had done for me and all he was showing me and all He was going to do for me in future days. For the first time in my life I noticed the tiny flowers growing in the earth, the blades of grass. I noticed the colours. The sky looked as if someone had taken soap and water and washed it blue.[2]

2. Irvine, *Witchcraft to Christ*, 144.

I find that the biographies of great lives tend not to linger very long at the hero's champagne moments. There appears to be a tendency to dwell on the trials and disappointments to the point where, even in a chapter about attaining some new success or happiness, it is with relish that the writer finishes the chapter with, ". . . but it was not to last."

Linger here we must. The hero's journey is increasingly punctuated with celebrations because it is increasingly punctuated with victories, and these will culminate in the final denouement.

The people of Israel were commanded to celebrate; commanded to rejoice and be glad. This was true for all three of their annual feasts but especially for the Feast of Tabernacles. This feast marked the Reward moment in their journey. Passover marked the crossing of the threshold, Pentecost came to mark the giving of the law at Sinai, the beginning of Israel's testing in the wilderness. Tabernacles marked the end of the testing, the entrance into the Promised Land, the sloughing off of their nomadic lifestyles to finally exchange it for the longed for sedentary life, each one dwelling under his vine and under his fig tree. The land flowing with milk and honey was theirs. They were commanded to mark this moment in their history every year and explain the reasons for it to their children.

## Ruminate

When Jewish singer Helen Shapiro[3] had her first encounters with Christian claims that Jesus was the Jewish Messiah, she had a lot to think about. She had been given a book written by Stan Telchin: *Betrayed*, which told the story of Telchin's initially hostile response to his daughter when she decided she believed in Jesus. Shapiro found herself entirely convinced by the astonishing number of ways in which Jesus of Nazareth fulfilled so many prophecies in the Hebrew Bible about the Messiah. But there were numerous stumbling blocks: the idea that she must become a "Christian"

---

3. She tells her own story in *Walking Back to Happiness*, 183.

from being a Jew, the terrible track record of anti-semitism on the part of those who claimed to be Christ's followers, the portrayals of Jesus as a white Westerner, the habit of referring to the Hebrew Bible as the "Old Testament," the sedate, dull, dreariness of so many English church services compared to the joyful noise of synagogue life. A defining, life-changing moment had come and she felt excited by her new discovery, but there was ruminating to do. She became involved in Messianic congregations. "They didn't see themselves as ex-Jews," she reminisces, "but Jews who had come to a fulfilment in Yeshua."[4] To be amongst them was to feel that she had come home.

Our crisis moment and the prize it has yielded has permanently changed our view of things, changed the whole reason why we do things or choose not to do them. For world class 400 Meter runner, Kriss Akabusi, his new found faith did not for a moment suggest to him that he give up athletics. It merely gave him a new reason to run. He now had "a new motive to succeed."[5] Though his achievements were great he felt convinced that he was not yet at the top of his game. Success for its own sake, however, meant nothing to him now. Success for the glory of God became a far more compelling idea. He came to faith in Christ in 1987 and with this new motive he made the bold move of learning a new event: the 400 meter hurdles, aiming to be the best in Britain that year. This involved intense training but Kriss had always been a very hard worker. Despite an untidy technique he achieved this. In 1988, he competed in the World Championships. He prayed before the race and felt God saying: "*You* can't do it, but just go out there and start."[6] He had been suffering with an injury: "I got to 120 metres and started to worry about my leg. The niggling pain came right back but I told myself to have faith. I carried on running. I made it and won a gold medal."[7] He reflected in an interview for the Christian press: "I go into competitions now and I've no worries

4. Ibid., 190.

5. Harrison, *Kriss Akabusi on Track*, 152.

6. Ibid., 179. Emphasis added.

7. Ibid., 180.

at all. I've just got to get onto the blocks and Jesus does the rest. It sounds stupid to a lay person, but it's not me that's winning . . . Now I'm running better than I have ever done in my career."[8]

For George Müller, the appraisal of what he was and had now become was rather more stark. It meant a clean break with his debauched past. The summer of 1829 was when his faltering Christian faith became firmly established as he flourished under the guidance of Henry Craik, a leading member of a brand new sect called the Brethren. Over that summer in Devonshire his life changed dramatically. "There was a day," reflected Müller, "when I died, utterly died, died to George Müller, his opinions, preferences; died to the approval or blame of even my brethren and friends—and since then I have studied only to show myself approved unto God."[9]

It seems that every great seeker after the purposes of God goes through a climactic moment in which, in desperation, their very life is handed over to God and the prize of some new power and peace is given in exchange.

Long before his famous founding of the China Inland Mission, James Hudson Taylor was acutely aware of his shortcomings but knew he could, by himself, do nothing about them: "Pray for me, my dear Amelia, pray for me," he wrote to his sister, "I am seeking entire sanctification. Oh, that I could take hold of the blessed promises of God's Holy Word. My heart longs for perfect holiness."[10] That evening the wrestling with God continued. He promised God he would "go anywhere, do anything"[11] if only God would answer him and keep him from falling. Suddenly something happened: "Never shall I forget the feeling that came over me then. Words can never describe it, I felt I was in the presence of God, entering into covenant with the Almighty. I felt as though I wished to withdraw my promise, but could not. Something seemed to say, 'Your prayer is answered, your conditions are accepted.'"[12]

8. Ibid., 179.
9. Whittaker, *Seven Great Prayer Warriors*, 9.
10. Ibid., 37.
11. Ibid.
12. Ibid.

ACT 2

However, this, it seems was not the end of his struggles. In 1869, in China, shortly after the birth of his fourth son to Maria his wife, we find him again in a state of dissatisfaction with his spiritual state. He wanted "unbroken communion with Christ,"[13] a happy state that Maria had been enjoying for years. A fellow missionary, John McCarthy, wrote to him advising him that the answer lay not in striving but in abiding, a state which, by its very nature, required none of *his* strength at all. He began to see that abiding in Christ could be seen as a fact regardless of how we feel: "If we are faithless, God remains faithful" (2 Tim.2:13) became one of his favorite verses. He explains: "Do we cease to abide in our homes when asleep at night?"[14] Abiding was a fact that one did not even need to be conscious of in order to benefit from. This new insight equipped him for the immense growth and renown of the China Inland Mission. In 1884, the famous Cambridge Seven volunteered for service there and by 1891 C.I.M was 500 strong and had a presence in every Chinese province doing good, caring for the sick and sharing Christ. It also kept him strong through the terrible reversals and tragedies that resulted from the Boxer rising of 1899.

Has something brought you to a crisis moment? Be sure to notice what you walked away with. Something of the old you was left behind but something of priceless importance was seized. You caught hold of a long sought after connectedness to God, a much needed power or peace. You fought and won and received a prize. You have seized the sword. It is time to celebrate this and think about what this means for the rest of your life on earth and into eternity.

### The Life of Christ:

His cry of "It is finished" John 19:30.

13. Ibid., 71.
14. Ibid., 72.

## Discussion:

1. Are you in a supreme and unprecedented struggle right now? What do you seek?

2. Have you been through a climactic struggle at some point in your life? Can you remember the greatest thing you gained from it?

# Act 3

# 3:1. The Journey Back

THE ADVENTURER IS PROPELLED by the final contest into the journey back. The land in which the ordeal has taken place has been a hostile one, as confirmed by the hero's recent encounter with the enemy. Now he or she must go home to share with loved ones the treasure or the elixir won through the long ordeal.

One of the most text book Journey Back moments in recent times is in the 2015 version of *Cinderella*, directed by Kenneth

Branagh, a film that, thanks to my two daughters, I am extremely familiar with. All the way through the story, Cinderella has been tested to the limit as to whether she will continue to live by her father's aphorism: "Have courage; be kind." After her father's death, loyalty to her parents' memory keeps her in the family home where she serves her extremely abusive stepmother who, following the death of Cinderella's father, can no longer afford to keep a household of servants and cooks so dismisses them all. She then forces Cinderella to do all their work. Following a chance encounter with her in the woods, the prince throws a ball for all the marriageable women in the kingdom in the hope that the mystery girl will come. By the time the stepmother and stepsisters have left for the prince's ball, having forbidden Cinderella to go, we find Cinderella sobbing and in her gravest danger yet of giving in to fear and hate instead of courage and kindness. Enter: the Fairy Godmother. Thanks to her transformations, Cinderella goes to the ball and seizes her prize by dancing with the prince. The Journey Back is triggered by the clock. She must get back home before the last bell strikes at the hour of midnight. She cuts off her conversation with the prince, who is as captivated by her as she is by him. She runs back to her carriage leaving behind, of course, a glass slipper. The bells are loudly chiming as she speeds home. Slowly the spell is wearing off. The horses are slowly turning back into mice as they gallop, the driver is changing back into a goose as he tries to drive the carriage as fast as he can, the footman is becoming a lizard once again and the carriage is slowly shrinking back into a pumpkin, its wheels becoming more and more useless as they turn back into pumpkin foliage. To add to the tension, a delegation of cavalry has been sent in pursuit bent on protecting the prince from this unknown girl that has turned his head so quickly, thinking it is all the plot of a rival kingdom. But the footman grows back his tail and by this he is able to release the catch that shuts an iron gate on the advancing cavalry.

Eventually, Cinderella must walk the rest of the way, soaked in pumpkin juice. She is back in her filthy rags now but filled with gladness and wonder at the evening's events. A final brush with evil is yet to come: the very next day the stepmother will realize that the mystery girl at the ball was none other than Cinderella.

It is this chase scene that is a classic Journey Back. In fictional stories, there is normally a need for a ramping up of the energy at this stage. The hero has got what they came for and all is well. The hero might even be tempted to stay where they are rather than go back. This could get quite boring for the audience who has already sat through such a long story.

Not only is the audience's attention at stake, however. The moral tone of the story needs elevating at this point. Some kind of trigger is needed to ensure that a wider world gets the benefit of what the hero has won. It is this part of the hero's journey that elevates the story from an individual victory into a breakthrough for humankind. In Cinderella's case it will be a victory for the whole kingdom of courage over fear and intrigue and of kindness over hateful abuse and plotting. Indeed, without this wider benefit we would never have a reason to call the main protagonist a hero at all. We do not call people heroes who have merely gained a great thing for themselves. There must, at the very least, be some inspiration to share with others who face the same foe.

For this overflow of blessing to happen, the hero must be propelled from the perils of self-congratulation and the attractions of the good life. If not, their finest hour could be their greatest undoing. They could end up going soft like the whiskey guzzling veterans whom we tend to meet at the start of Act II. They are the once valiant stars of historic death defying feats that still possess extraordinary skills but have lost their edge. They are re-recruited for the hero's team in the hope that their long dormant genius will again prove useful in some new venture. They are gruff and obstinate as the hero tries to knock them back into shape.

The difficulty for us with the Journey Back episode is that often it is little more than a screen writer's tool. It is necessary for the narrative but ends up being the part of the story that least resembles real life. The writer takes the gamble that the audience's lust for excitement will be greater than their desire for believability at this stage. They have suspended their incredulity this long; a little excess of the fantastical will not hurt, just to get the story moving along. But, of course, in real life, we mostly do not get ourselves into car chases, and we do not regularly need to take cover while an enormous complex that had been the home of an evil regime, finally blows up. Still less likely is it that we will ever find ourselves chased from a castle in a pumpkin carriage. So what, if anything, does a Journey Back look like in real life?

A good place to start is to say that, for the unfinished biblical story of salvation, this is the beginning of the most important part. It is our cue. It is the start of our part. There has been a victory at Calvary. Christ's resurrection has triggered the Great Commission: the sending of the Church into all the world with the good news to tell. Then, the ascension triggered the outpouring of the Spirit and the empowerment of the Church to do this well. The global Church is central to Act III in the unfinished story of God's conquest of evil. The Church has been propelled into the world to bring the wider benefits of the victory of Christ. All the time, evil is still at large and will gather its forces for the final denouement at the end of the age. The return of Christ will be the final conquest of evil bringing about the new heaven and the new earth. Until then, there is news to tell.

The very first occurrence in the Bible of the phrase, "good news" is when four lepers have ventured out from the walls of the besieged city of Samaria to find that the enemy encampment is now deserted. The soldiers have left behind an abundance of food and wine. The lepers begin to feast when their consciences awaken them to the fact that the whole city is starving to death while they gorge themselves. They say, "This is a day of *good news*. We cannot keep this to ourselves" (2Kings 7:9). They go and alert the royal household to the news that the siege has been mysteriously lifted, something that Elisha the prophet had already predicted would happen. Truly good news is the kind of news that, if we were to keep it to ourselves, we would suffer a stricken conscience.

In the history of the Christian faith, the long dormant missionary urge to bring the good news to the world was initially reawakened by the discovery of the Americas and other far off lands. Ignatius of Loyola was not slow to seize the opportunity and formed the Society of Jesus with the pope's blessing in 1540. However, the impetus behind what we often refer to as the Age of Missions was the revival phenomena of the eighteenth century. Once awakened by the Spirit it became morally unacceptable for thoughtful Christians to keep such joys to themselves. Jonathan Edwards, leader of what is rightly termed the Great Awakening in Northampton, New England, started the conversation with his succinctly titled tract of 1748: *An Humble Attempt to Promote Explicit Agreement and Visible Union of God's People in Extraordinary Prayer for the Revival of Religion and the Advancement of Christ's Kingdom on Earth*. A cobbler from Northampton, England came across this and was deeply influenced by it. This man was William Carey. In 1792, he wrote his epoch-making: *An Enquiry into the Obligations of Christians to Use Means for the Conversion of the Heathen*. With Carey, the Baptist Missionary Society was born and he, with his wife Dorothy, set sail for India, blazing a trail for a hundred years and more of similar efforts. He saw the spreading of "the knowledge of the glad tidings" as the "solemn responsibility" of all Christians.[1]

In time, many who had not received the call to go on overseas mission were similarly stirred, sometimes from great ease and privilege, to stand up for the people on their very doorstep, people such as Lord Shaftesbury and "Dr. Barnardo." G.K. Chesterton made his mark on the arts after coming to faith at Slade School of Art where he had led a bohemian life in the 1890s.

In 1924, Eric Liddell won the 400 meter gold medal in the Paris Olympics, breaking the then world record of 47.6 seconds.[2] The very next year, Liddell left his native Scotland for China to take up a teaching post there in obedience to Christ, a decision that would see him captured by the Japanese during the war and end his days as a prisoner in 1945. Through it all, his life was characterized by honest, straightforward speaking and action:

> Let us put ourselves before ourselves and look at ourselves. The bravest moment of a person's life is the moment when he looks at himself objectively without

1. Myers, *William Carey*, 26.
2. Johnson, *Eric H. Liddell*, 54.

wincing, without complaining. . . What am I going to do about what I see? The action called for is surrender—of ourselves to God.[3]

In more recent times Sarah de Carvalho left the glamor of a job in TV working with all the stars in 1988 to pursue a call to go and work among the street children of Brazil. The very moment she made this decision, some very attractive offers of work in television came her way. She fought temptation, turned them down and went. Finally, full of excitement, she arrived in Brazil in March 1991 and said these priceless words to the Lord: "What lies ahead only You know. This time You are the producer, writer and director. The script is in Your hand."[4]

The Journey Back also has many affinities with what the psychologist Elliott Jacques first described as the "mid-life crisis."[5] Catholic theologian Gerald O' Collins rightly prefers the more positive-sounding "Second Journey,"[6] the journey from maturity to old age. It is the "afternoon of life."[7] I will let you fill in for yourself what the first and third journeys are. This second journey, which can begin in our thirties, forties or fifties, is usually the most generative and successful period of our lives. However, we are often propelled into that generativity by the anxiety and unease that comes from resting atop a set of achievements made in the morning of life that start to feel empty. You've got a PhD: so what? You've got a successful business: and? You've got a dream home: big deal. A state of alarm comes over us and we set off again, on a new journey with clarified goals. We set out on this journey having set our compass in a new direction. This often happens in the

---

3. Woodbridge (ed) *More than Conquerors*, 226.

4. Carvakho, *Street Children of Brazil*, 43.

5. Jacques, "Death and the Mid-Life Crisis."

6. O'Collins, *Second Journey*. There is, in any case, no consensus that mid-life necessarily leads to a crisis at all: Squires, "Midlife Without a Crisis," Page Z20. Accessed online 25 August 2016: http://www.washingtonpost.com/wp-srv/health/seniors/stories/midlife042099.htm

7. O'Collins, *Second Journey*, 4, citing Carl Jung, *Psychological Reflections*, 137–8.

wake of a journey inwards, which, though terribly lonely, eventually opens us outwards to others with renewed empathy.

As I say, at the beginning of the journey, we normally find ourselves unseated in some way from the ideals and values that got us to where we are. Here is O'Collins:

> Very many people choose external goals to define their existence. They aim at becoming head of their department in the public service, a bishop in a large diocese, secretary to their trade union, principal of a high school, a journalist for a leading newspaper or some other 'top' person. They move upward in society and then one of two things may happen to them in their thirties, forties or fifties: (1) they reach their goal and it bores them, or (2) they realize that they may never attain it and panic sets in.[8]

This realization, as it slowly dawns, can be extremely disorienting. Old certainties are radically questioned. People going through this develop a desire to "try themselves out again."[9] Mother Teresa felt, at this point, a "call within a call.[10] She was happily stationed at the Bengal Mission of the Loreto sisters, a quiet and peaceful place with a beautiful garden. Then, while on a journey from Calcutta to Darjeeling in 1946—she was in her mid-thirties at the time—she distinctly felt that God was calling her to ". . . a vocation to give up even Loreto where I was very happy and to go out in the streets to serve the poorest of the poor."[11] Within two years, she had made this happen and walked alone for the first time out into the streets of Calcutta. The rest is history.

John Henry Newman's second journey was sparked by a serious illness. In 1833, he was alone on the island of Sicily. His fever became so severe that he thought he would die. Recovering from this brought an entirely new lease of life. His journey back home would be a time in which he sensed a new call to a significant new

8. O'Collins, *Second Journey*, 58.

9. O'Collins, *Second Journey*, 14.

10. Muggeridge, *Something Beautiful for God*, 62.

11. Ibid.

sphere of ministry in England. On the ship he penned the now immortal words:

Lead, Kindly Light, amid the encircling gloom,
Lead Thou me on!
The night is dark, and I am far from home—
Lead Thou me on!
Keep Thou my feet; I do not ask to see
The distant scene—one step enough for me.

I was not ever thus, nor prayed that Thou
Shouldst lead me on.
I loved to choose and see my path; but now
Lead Thou me on!
I loved the garish day, and spite of fears,
Pride ruled my will: remember not past years.[12]

What we seek as we set off on the Journey Back is probably best described by Rabbi Harold Kushner. He himself experienced a degree of fame and fortune when his first book: *When Bad Things Happen to Good People*,[13] about the death of his 14 year old son, became an international best-seller, defying all expectations. This sudden and monumental success triggered for him his own second journey and the insights he gained were recorded in his second book: *When All You've Ever Wanted Isn't Enough.*[14] He says this:

> Our souls are not hungry for fame, comfort, wealth, or power. Those rewards create almost as many problems as they solve. Our souls are hungry for meaning, for the sense that we have figured out how to live so that our lives matter, so the world will be at least a little bit different for our having passed through it. . . . Would our disappearance leave the world poorer, or just less crowded?[15]

12. Cited in O'Colllins, *Second Journey*, 37–8.
13. Kushner, *When Bad Things Happen to Good People*.
14. Harold Kushner, *When All You've Ever Wanted Isn't Enough*.
15. Kushner, *When All You've Ever Wanted Isn't Enough*, 18.

So, a screen writer's ploy becomes a vital episode in the salvation story and a fiction-writer's strategy for injecting some excitement into a story turns out to be an episode that a great many of us enter into, willingly or not, during the afternoon of our lives. It is at this point that the gains of the central crisis stand a chance of being enjoyed by a wider world and it is at this point that the central crisis turns out to have been a mid-life reassessment of what truly matters, which the Journey Back will take us towards.

Are you ready for God to commission you, to send you off in a new direction that ensures that what you have gained will not be for your benefit alone?

## The Life of Christ:

His Great Commission: Matthew 28:18–20.

## Discussion:

1. Have you been stirred by a desire to take part in God's mission into the world? What obstacles do you face?

2. Are you reassessing the goals that you once thought were the be-all-and-end-all? What conclusions are you reaching?

# 3:2. The Final Test

STORIES ONLY HAVE THREE basic moods: preparation, conflict and celebration. In the hero's journey Act I is dominated by preparation, Act II by conflict and Act III by celebration. However, within each act, there is a continual shift from one mood to another. Even in Act I, there are many conflict elements: the Refusal of the Call, for instance. In Act II there are many minor victories and celebrations culminating in The Approach. And in Act III there are elements of preparation and conflict. In fact, it is in the final denouement that preparation and conflict both reach their high water mark.

This will be the final preparatory test—this time preparing the hero for re-entry. And this will be the final conflict—the last ditch effort of the evil forces to foil the hero's plan.

Our expectations of on-screen heroes is very high. After they have gone through an ordeal that would leave most people traumatized, we watch dissatisfied unless all that they seem to have learned from their ordeal is tested out. We want to know: have they really changed? This episode meets that demand by means of a second fight. Its form will be similar to the crisis: there will be a kind of a death and resurrection, and a catharsis but the implications will be broad.[1] We are continuing with the elevated moral tone secured by the previous episode. This fight will not only be the hero's fight: it will be humanity's fight. It is the moment when, just when we thought that the evil citadel was destroyed, the hero discovers a ticking bomb powerful enough to wipe out an entire population. Evil has been dealt a decisive blow but its central power somehow gains a new and monstrous energy, like the Sea Witch Ursula who turns into a gigantic octopus in the closing scenes of Walt Disney's *The Little Mermaid* or the dragonesque proportions that Maleficent takes on just prior to her demise.

Because the audience has already seen the hero obtain what they came for and begin their return to the ordinary world, there is a great resilience by now. The audience thinks the hero cannot die. The reader is already poised to celebrate a comic ending. Writers, therefore, tend to try especially hard to shock the audience one last time. The writer is being trusted to deliver on the expected "happily ever after" but will play around with that trust at this stage, like a cat with a mouse.

This episode often involves these two elements:

1. Vogler, *Writer's Journey*, 199.

## Act 3

# Jeopardy for the Whole Adventure

In romantic comedies, we find the girl just about to say her vows to the wrong guy at the altar. Will her real suitor make it in time to stop the ceremony? He has learned the hard way how foolish he had been to let her go and now we want to know whether he can deliver on the lessons he has learned, boldly risking everything to get her back.

In real life, achieving a final victory for humanity can end up hanging in the balance for decades and is not swiftly over in tears of sentiment. For Nelson Mandela there must have been moments when it looked like it was all over. He freely admitted that, at the time of his sentencing to life imprisonment in 1962, he believed in violent struggle and seethed with anger against whites. He had strong sympathies with an "ultra revolutionary stream of African nationalism,"[2] and was a leader in the MK, the armed wing of the African National Congress, which was committed to acts of sabotage against the state, though even then only at times and places where harm to people could be kept to a minimum. He was far from being a terrorist. While in prison, a deepening commitment to forgiveness and reconciliation developed: "In prison, my anger towards whites decreased, but my hatred for the system grew. I wanted South Africa to see that I loved even my enemies, while I hated the system that turned us against one another."[3] This even extended to the invitation to three of his prison wardens to attend his presidential inauguration on 10 May 1994, four years after his release.

The lesson he had learned was clear: "To make peace with an enemy, one must work with that enemy . . . and that enemy becomes your partner."[4] This leads us into the next key feature of this episode.

## Demonstrating New Credentials

We stay in the continent of Africa but travel North to what would today be called Algeria, and look at the life of a man of Berber

2. Cited in Frost, *Struggling to Forgive*, 3.
3. Ibid., 6.
4. Ibid., 2.

86

descent: Augustine of Hippo. His mother was devout—and prayed for him constantly—while he was on a mission to enjoy himself as much as possible. His relatively well-to-do background allowed him a frivolous and often immoral life in which, by his late teens, he was bent on competing with the sexual exploits of his dissolute friends. He found himself swimming more and more in "hell's black river of lust,"[5] culminated in a lengthy but doomed love affair with a woman of Carthage by whom he had a son. By the age of thirty he was still "floundering in the same quagmire"[6] Then, one day in 386 his torment brought him to utter despair. He felt that he was a total captive to his appetites. He was in a garden with his dear friend Alypius and was becoming deeply sad. He went somewhere private to sob to himself when he heard a child singing the words "Take up and read, take up and read." He duly took up a copy of the Scriptures and, turning to Paul's Letter to the Romans, read the words: "Not in reveling and drunkenness, not in lust and wantonness, not in quarrels and rivalries. Rather, arm yourselves with the Lord Jesus Christ; spend no more thought on nature and nature's appetites." The effect was instant: ". . . as I came to the end of the sentence, it was as though the light of confidence flooded into my heart and all the darkness of doubt was dispelled."[7]

Thus was born within Augustine a new life that would make him into the most influential post-biblical theologian of all time, whose contributions have ranged from being the originator of just war theory (the antecedent of the Geneva Convention) to giving us some enduring insights about God as love and God as Trinity. God is, according to Augustine, a being consisting of love relationships: He is the Lover, the Beloved and the Love between them: Father, Son and Holy Spirit. He made large strides in trying to define the relationship between Church and State. He is even credited with being, to some extent, the founder of individualism. His *Confessions* is a piece of work of a kind that was virtually unheard of at the time: a spiritual autobiography. Until then, people had not

5. Augustine, *Confessions* III, 1.
6. Augustine, *Confessions* VI, 2.
7. Augustine, *Confessions* VII, 12.

ACT 3

thought about their relationship to God in such private, intimate, individual terms. However, perhaps the one thing that permeated his life was his emphasis on God's grace, God's underserved favor towards people like himself. He never forgot the unfathomable mercy that met him in his early thirties and released him from the terrible chains that bound his soul.

His chance to demonstrate this profound appreciation for God's mercy and love was not slow in coming. Within a few years, Augustine, having made the most remarkable progress, was installed as the Bishop of Hippo. Early on in his ministry, a controversy escalated around a fellow bishop by the name of Donatus. His followers were referred to as the Donatists. Their grudge went back quite a few decades to the Great Persecution of AD303–13. This persecution of the Christians was the last of the organized persecutions of the Roman Empire. It was also the worst and caught many Christians off guard because there had been a long time of relative peace preceding it. Not everyone was a hero and many freely surrendered their Scriptures to the authorities and renounced Christ. When peace returned, they desired to renew their faith. Some even went on to hold office. As the decades wore on a large part of the North African church reacted strongly against bishops who had been *traditores* or 'traitors,' and refused to acknowledge the validity of any ordinations they carried out, spurning the ministries of any clergy that had been ordained by a *traditore*. By the 390s, the problem had still not gone away but Augustine knew exactly what his rule of thumb would be: convey love.[8] He identified exactly what their problem was: a lack of love. For many years, he addressed it head on, helping to define the true Christian faith over against intolerant bigotry. In this extract is one of Augustine's most famous sayings:

> Once for all, then, a short precept is given thee: Love, and do what thou wilt: whether thou hold thy peace, through love hold thy peace; whether thou cry out, through love cry out; whether thou correct, through love correct; whether thou spare, through love do thou spare: let the

8. Park, "Lacking Love or Conveying Love?"

root of love be within, of this root can nothing spring but what is good.[9]

A life once filled with utter revulsion at himself had been taken over by love. He had become an apostle of grace.

Fred Lemon was a man with a hot temper and an enormous capacity to seethe with hatred. In 1920, at the age of five, he had been taken into a home for boys, along with his brother, his mother being too desperately poor to keep all four of her children. She had been harsh and often drunk yet he missed her terribly in his own single bed after having been so accustomed to the warmth of an entire family sleeping together. She never wrote, never visited and sent nothing at Christmas. Later, as a young man in the East End of London he took to a life of crime. Petty thefts progressed to organized raids. Soon enough the law caught up with him and, leaving behind a loyal wife and three neglected children, he ended up in the notorious Dartmoor Prison. His labor in the mornings was to sew post bags under the watchful eye of a prison warden whom he especially hated known as Tojo. Most wardens were fair and professional. Tojo was one of a small list of wardens that were incessantly sarcastic and vindictive. Fred developed a deepening loathing toward him.

On Sundays chapel attendance in the prison was very high simply because it was a break from the monotony and boredom. One Sunday, Fred decided to go to the Methodist chapel service instead of the Anglican one simply because he was plotting to escape and needed the help of a prisoner who went to the Methodist service. However, the chaplain, Percy Holmes, was different to all the others: not in robes but dressed in ordinary clothes, and not remote or posh but friendly and approachable with a round face and a kind smile. In fact, more than anything, it was a sincere handshake from Percy as Fred entered the chapel that was the single tiny catalyst that would begin to set Fred's life on an entirely different course. That one handshake made Fred, whose life was filled only with darkness, suspicion and hate, feel that he mattered, that he was respected.

9. *Homilies on the First Epistle of John 7.8*, cited in Park, "Lacking Love or Conveying Love? 118.

As Fred sat down, he found himself leaning forward, transfixed by a message that was easy to understand and seemed relevant to him and his worries and cares. He immediately arranged for regular visits to his cell from Percy. Fred began reading the Bible and his heart began to change. He wrote to his wife, Doris, asking her to forgive all the pain he had put her through, and he suddenly lost his persistent stammer.

However, neither his fellow inmates nor his wardens were going to let him off very lightly for having "got religion." The change in him was so sudden that the wardens were suspicious, especially when his stammer disappeared. They suspected he had been faking the stammer and had now stopped as part of some carefully planned trick. He found himself in solitary confinement for three weeks for an offence he was wholly innocent of. His little gas light was smashed in so that he could no longer see to read his Bible at night. Former friends turned against him. Some even made him fall from the top of a 15 foot ladder while he was on painting duty, ripping the cartilage in his knee and causing months of pain. This injury also ensured that he was soon back in the workshop with Tojo stitching post bags. Fred knew that in his heart he still hated the wardens, especially Tojo. That murderously hot temper of his, so marvelously contained until now, was ready to boil over. One night, in August 1950, despairing of his Christian faith, and with Percy Holmes away for a few weeks, he resolved that he would kill Tojo the next day. He would do it with one of the cutting knives that were used in the workshop. At last he would be free from the relentless provocation. Then he would doubtless be hanged, Tojo would be replaced and Doris, the only person that would miss him, would at least be free to find a better husband and father to their children than he had been.

That very night, three men suddenly appeared in his locked cell, their faces hard to see. The man on the right pointed to the man in the center and said, "Fred, this is Jesus." This central figure then spoke to Fred at length about his entire life up until now, concluding with the warning: "If you want to become a Christian, you must drive the hatred from your heart."[10] Then, the three figures began to fade from view and with an audible "click" disappeared. Fred felt no fear but only a deep peace and went to sleep. The next morning, perhaps surprisingly, his intentions had not changed. He took his seat at the table in the workshop as usual and started stitching but his anger was reaching boiling point as he listened to Tojo's horrible voice barking out orders. Fred began staring at Tojo for so long and with such rage that, for the first time ever, he could see fear in the face of the warden. By now Fred had grabbed the cutting knife and the entire workshop fell silent as all the men watched the stand-off. Suddenly, Fred's arm went completely numb. He was unable to move the knife. "Get on with your work,"[11] Tojo said, trying to conceal his terror but sensing that Jack would not follow through on the attack. "I knew as surely as anything," recalls Fred, "that it had been God himself who had held my arm back from doing that terrible deed."[12]

Percy the chaplain had repeatedly counselled Fred to forgive the Wardens and to pray for them but it was not until the Christmas of that year that he finally fell to his knees and said to God:

> It's Christmas! And I can't give you anything except my heart, so I give you that for the rest of my life. Come and cut this great lump of hatred out of it, will you? Tell me how I can forgive the screws. Show me how I can even *want* to forgive them. Listen—I'll tell you their nicknames for a start: Monkey, Fatty, Pig, Tojo.[13]

It wasn't until he spoke that last name to God, in a faltering and feeble attempt to forgive, that it happened. He felt the lump of hatred melt "like warmed snow."[14]

He was soon released and wonderfully reunited with his family, but there would continue to be tests of his temper. He got

---

10. Lemon & Knowlton, *Breakout*, 109–10.
11. Ibid., 111.
12. Ibid.
13. Ibid., 117.
14. Ibid., 118.

fired from his first job when, under severe provocation about his Christian faith, he took a man by the legs and threw him down a grain chute. The worst taunts came when he got a job in an office: "It was like Dartmoor all over again."[15] Many of the taunts weren't said to his face but in his hearing. They had learned of his criminal record and used this to pour derision on all that he had been saying about his faith in Christ. Previously, they had been lining up to tell him their troubles and ask for prayer. Now they called him a jail bird. During one tirade aired right behind him about Jesus being a myth, a conjuror and full of mumbo-jumbo, Fred could hardly keep himself in his seat:

> My old ticker was bursting. I half-rose in my chair; my fists were clenched and I was sweating freely. I'd show them! I'd teach them . . . Clearly and unmistakably, a voice spoke to me. 'Vengeance is mine,' it said. I sank back in my chair and let my heart's pounding subside. It was not for me to seek revenge for God. My part was to go on doing my job to the best of my ability, in whatever circumstances. Picking up my pen, I bent over my desk.[16]

The final denouement in our adventures will have these kinds of qualities. Everything seems to reach a new kind of climax just when we had thought our worst battles were over. All that we have gained seems suddenly to hang in the balance. It is a normally brief but critical test and its effect is to set the seal on what we will bring back to the ordinary world.

Fred went on to be in demand as a speaker and went beyond forgiving wardens to working with a class of people he had once hated even more: the police, and became active in the ministry of the Christian Police Association.

15. Ibid., 145.
16. Ibid., 145–6.

## The Life of Christ:

The Great Tribulation and Christ's triumphant return:
   Matthew 24.

## Discussion:

You thought it was all over but you are face to face with your old enemy. Does it help if you look upon this as your final exam, your last test to make sure you are ready to be the blessing to the world that God has gifted and prepared you to be?

# 3:3. The Return with the Elixir

THE MOMENT OF CLOSURE has arrived. In films and fairy tales alike, there is a sense that the story has now come full circle. It's when you are back to where you were before that you realize you have truly changed; and that's the whole point of the adventure. The mark of a true adventure is that the hero emerges transformed, freed from the things that once confused his or her priorities.

The task is a simple one: for the hero to make sure that the gains of the adventure are shared with everyone.

Archbishop Desmond Tutu's position has always been precarious. He has chosen the role of mediator, which means that he has given himself the impossible task of keeping both sides in a conflict happy enough to keep talking. There were many times when one party was angry at him for not opposing something they wanted him to speak out on. There were other times when the other party found him too outspoken and offensive. This role also meant that, when powerful political authorities did finally move into center stage and talk directly with each other, it was time for him to bow out gracefully. One of his early biographers captured this beautifully, even before the full fruits of his labors were seen:

> His strength is that the ultimate liberation of his people
> is more important than his own prestige and power. It
> is like Moses reaching the mountain top and seeing the
> promised land, but saying, 'I am not here to do the lead-
> ing, but to share the vision.'[1]

It is this quality that makes the true hero shine. The true hero returns with the booty of the adventure only to share it. Heroes share what they have seen. They share what they have learned. They share the joy of what they have become.

José Henriquez was one of the 33 miners caught up in the famous Chilean mine disaster of August 5—October 13, 2010. He and his coworkers had been trapped down a one hundred and twenty one year old gold and copper mine in Copiapo, San Jose, which had been unsafe for some time. Following a 69-day rescue operation, and with much prayer being offered up by the families and their churches, all 33 miners were miraculously rescued alive. During that time Henriquez, already an active preacher, had taken it on himself to provide spiritual comfort and guidance to the men who, from one day to the next, did not know whether they

1. Boulay, *Tutu*, 264.

would live to see their families again. In the heat of the mine shaft, 2,300 feet underground, Henriquez led 22 of the men through to a deep commitment to follow Christ and they all regularly joined in prayer. Coming back up to the surface in a specially designed NASA pod and being reunited with family was rightly greeted by many onlookers as a miracle. The President of Chile himself said, "Faith has moved mountains."[2] However, for Henriquez, this incredible rescue was only the start:

> Anyone might think that after managing to get out of the mine alive the story would be over. Usually that is how a movie ends. Our goal had been achieved, our objective reached, and now we had come to the finale. . . but a new story had begun.[3]

He soon found himself catapulted into an international ministry that would take him to a prayer breakfast at the White House with President Obama, a tour of Britain and Ireland where hundreds thronged cathedrals to hear him speak, and hundreds responded to the offer of salvation, and a trip to Israel on the invitation of the Israeli government.

Bono, Edge and Larry of U2 were involved, since their late teens, in charismatic expressions of Christianity which blew apart the hard divisions between Protestant and Catholic that were so familiar a feature of Dublin. Like many of their contemporaries, these young men were restless for something more authentic than the traditional churches were offering. Their involvement with the charismatic Shalom Fellowship grew more intense at the same time that their band was steadily rising to fame in the early 1980s. Their album *Boy*, had achieved critical acclaim and mesmerizing stage performances in the US and Britain were winning the allegiance of a growing fan base. In Dublin, their fame had already attracted a number of new members to Shalom, especially girls. However, it became increasingly difficult to keep U2 the band and

2. Pappas, "To Hell and Back: How 69 Days Underground Affects Spirituality."Accessed online 25 August 2016: http://www.nbcnews.com/id/39658360/ns/health-behavior/#.V7b4_SgrLIU

3. Henriquez, *Miracle in the Mine*, 133.

their commitment to the Shalom Fellowship in harmony. They had resolved within themselves that they could find ways to deal with the contradictions inherent between rock n' rock culture and a whole-hearted commitment to Christianity, but many in their congregation had graver doubts. These doubts intensified following a supposed prophecy from one of the members that they were to give up the band. The Shalom group placed a great emphasis on surrendering the ego and choosing the path of humility. Their first encounter with Phil Lynott at a concert where both U2 and Lynott's Thin Lizzy were part of the program only served to confirm their own growing doubts. Indeed, within four years, Lynott's heroin addiction would lead to his death at the age of 36. The band recorded an entire album: *October*, with this dilemma hanging over them. To add to the difficulty of the situation, neither the bass-player, Adam Clayton, nor their manager shared their Christian faith.

The whole world can be thankful that their deliberations led neither to the end of U2, nor to the abandonment of a distinctively faith-inspired artistic content and social conscience. Most impressive of all, perhaps, is this early description of their philosophy as a band:

> The exploitation and self-indulgence that was the fruit of fame would in U2's case be denied, forbidden. No sex, no drugs, no groupies, no orgies. Their band, their organization, would lead a revolution against the old tradition. And on all fronts; audiences would be respected, not abused by bulky minders. U2 shows would give value for money . . . There would be no excess, no decadence, nothing cheap or degrading . . . their lives, their music, their band, would bridge the gap between the rock n' roll they loved and the Christian ethos they were committed to.[4]

Actor David Suchet, otherwise known as Inspector Poirot, found faith while languishing in a lonely hotel room in Seattle having landed the part of a psychopathic killer in a Spielberg movie. The prestige of being in a Spielberg movie was a dream come true for him at that time but the battles in his mind about the existence

4. Duffy, *Unforgettable Fire*, 213.

ACT 3

of a spiritual realm were intensifying. He developed an overpowering desire to read a Bible. He found a Gideon Bible and could not put it down. He was enthralled by the life that was offered in the Gospels, and by Paul's teaching in certain remarkable passages such as Romans chapter 8. He connected with a pastor in America who ministered to him through a period in which he found himself being emotionally churned up and constantly crying. Soon, there was the familiar euphoria of finding freedom in Christ. But there were also the many challenges to face of being a Christian in that profession. For a start, being a celebrity church member suddenly placed him in demand at evangelistic events when his own faith still needed nurturing. Then there were the challenges of what his faith would allow him to portray on screen:

> As an actor I have to remain open to portray any type of character, even the unpleasant ones. In the story of Christ, someone has to play the part of the prostitute, and the soldiers who put the nails in His hands. The real test is whether the part glorifies evil or exposes it. As Christians we are called to be lights, but we can only be lights in the darkness. If by playing an unsavoury part in a film I can show the destruction that evil can bring into our lives, I feel I am being a light in that situation.[5]

The name "Guinness" has meant different things to different people. Primarily, of course, it is associated with the distinct Irish stout which achieved international success from the late 1700s. Then there is the *Guinness Book of Records* which began in 1955 as a way of promoting the brand. Many today have read at least one of the many books by American thinker and writer Os Guinesss, the great, great, great, grandson of Guinness founder Arthur Guinness. Others have encountered branches of the Guinness dynasty in fashion, banking, politics and philanthropy. Though not every heir to the name has worn it well, most have, it seems.

What is less well known is the deep religious faith of the earlier parts of the dynasty. In fact, the very existence of Guinness as a beer owes its origins to an Anglican Archbishop in Ireland leaving

5. Gidney, *In the Limelight*, 184.

some money in his will to his godson, Arthur Guinness, which was used to finance the brewing of beer. The archbishop would have been more than happy with this since in all parts of the British Isles alcoholism was spreading from drinking cheap Gin. Policies were being pursued that involved encouraging the poor to drink beer instead: much less alcoholic and believed at the time to be nutritious. Arthur himself was a devout Christian and an outspoken and generous philanthropist.[6]

Of particular significance to me have been the very many clergymen and missionaries that have been part of the Guinness line.[7] Henry Gratton Guinness was an enthusiastic evangelist and missionary and had been a popular preacher in the Ulster Revival of 1859. Having already founded Harley College in London, which he co-led with the famous Dr Barnado, in 1883 he acquired a very grand mansion house from Elizabeth Hulme called Cliff House in Derbyshire, England. She donated it to him to help further his missionary training work. He called it Hulme Cliffe College. In 1904, he sold it to the Wesleyan Methodist Church and it became known as Cliff College. It expanded to become a center for Spirit-filled Christianity attracting thousands to its annual festivals including Billy Graham—and Fred Lemon whom we heard from earlier. One of its principals, Howard Belben, had also been the minister of Wolverhampton Methodist Church where my grandfather and my uncle Paul were members and regular attenders at Cliff College festivals. That uncle and his wife prayed so insistently for my family that, out-of-the-blue, my brother became a Christian while at university. Then, even more unexpectedly, I became a Christian in 1988 when I was a long-haired art student experimenting with drugs. The effect of Christ entering my life was so dramatic that all my interests changed and I developed a growing fascination with the Bible and with theology. I taught myself Greek and made an attempt at Hebrew. I ventured to do a correspondence degree course

6. http://listverse.com/2015/02/05/10-strange-stories-about-the-fascinating-guinness-family/ [Accessed online 25 August 2016].

7. The story of the religious Guinness line is told by Michele Guinness, *The Guinness Legend.*

in theology and loved it. This led to a part time MA, which led to a PhD, which led to my first job in academia managing a theological graduate school. Then, in 2012, Cliff College advertised for a Lecturer in Theology—and here I am. Thanks Henry Gratton Guinness, and thanks Uncle.

# Conclusion

ONE OF THE REASONS given for early publisher rejections of this book at proposal stage was that the readers would be looking for biblical narratives to base their lives on, not fictional story-lines. I did increase the biblical content but I am aware that, even now, I could be accused of encouraging people to set the compass of their lives by Hollywood. I could be understood as recommending that people no longer treat films and novels as escapism but should learn to take them more seriously, to actually navigate their way through the challenges of life using Indiana Jones, or that they should brighten the dullness of their week by acting like Neo the hero trapped within a computer simulation. I could be construed as saying that, instead of picking up the Bible, my readers should open a nearby copy of a John Grisham crime novel or a Stephen King thriller, and take their cues from the lead character, whoever they may be. Perhaps even a heist story like *Oceans Eleven* will do: forgetting for now the eighth Commandment.

Part of the problem here lies in what fiction has become. The effect of the big screen has been a move away from the realism of the early eighteenth century novels, the first books to be called novels. Besides novels there were the Romances. These were more fantastical tales, tales of wonder that were a good deal less anchored in what life is really like. While the Romance never finally fell out of vogue, the big screen has given us a new fantastical appetite. Even realist novels when adapted for the screen can accrue so much in the way of poetic license that the result is as thrilling as a Romance. Most popular films are a kind of Romance. But there is another thing that has been lost. The first novels were rooted in the tradition of the moral lesson. They were rooted in a culture that was Christian and in that culture stories were told of virtue in the face of temptation, perseverance in the face of trial and just deserts coming upon evil doers. Today, fiction often retains this moral lesson—one of the commonest underlying messages in today's stories is "crime doesn't pay." But there are many other messages, such as, "Learn to be true to yourself," or "Sometimes what you need is right under your nose." And, while we are certainly expected to learn life skills from these stories, the lessons are offered in a very indirect way. Early novels had a much more direct feel and a more high-minded moral tone (think of Dickens for instance).

What I am doing here is rehydrating for Christian use something that is of ostensibly Christian origins: the realistic moral tale. The baroque excesses of romance and sentiment that have poured into our lives from Hollywood, together with the unattainable omnicompetence of its super-slick heroes is something I part company with. This is why I have packed this little book with illustrations drawn from very real, often very fallible, lives.

This book is my first experiment with what I'm calling Regenerative Correlation. This is what I mean by "rehydrating." I am partly inspired by Don Browning's Revised Correlation, which is a way of bringing Christianity and culture into a mutually beneficial and mutually critical dialogue.[8] I am also inspired by a phrase of theologian John Milbank that describes how so often secular ideas in the West turn out to be a reshaped version of something that was originally Christian but which has kept better pace with culture than the original version has: ". . . the distortions develop

---

8. His key work was *A Fundamental Practical Theology*. See also Lynch, *Understanding Theology and Popular Culture*.

better certain aspects of orthodoxy which orthodoxy must then later recoup."[9] This is part of the wider aims of the "Radical Orthodoxy" that he inspired. It is an intellectual movement which ". . . attempts to reclaim the world by situating its concerns and activities within a theological framework."[10] This book has been my first attempt at doing that. I have re-Christianized the moral tale—improved as it has been in so many ways by Campbell, Vogler and the on-going output of novels and films—and illustrated it *from* real life *for* real life. I have re-situated the adventure story, the monomyth "within a theological framework." I've put God back where he belongs, if you will.

Lastly, nothing of what I outline here is prescriptive. All of it is suggestive. I do not for a moment think that it will be possible to neatly package your life, or any part of it, into the twelve episodes. Trust me, I've tried. What I hope this book has been is a navigational tool for use during those times when we are in the thick of one of the three basic moods: preparation, conflict, celebration. This book has tried to bring clarity about what you can expect to come next, what the present moment is for, what the past has been leading up to, and, perhaps most importantly, what to do. Then, I've reinforced that by indexing this guidance to the life of Christ himself.

Perhaps, in a small group setting this has all been a great conversation and prayer starter. Perhaps in solitary reflections, some thoughts have been confirmed and you have been encouraged to take a step you knew you should take but just needed permission.

Whatever the benefit, I would love to hear from you.

Godspeed on the hero's path as you follow the greatest Hero of them all.

9. Milbank, *Theology and Social Theory*, xv. I don't, for a moment, believe that Milbank would approve of what I'm doing here, by the way. He is a purist and resists all forms of "correlationist" theology, but I find it impossible to resist having a go at doing something like this with his ideas.

10. Milbank, Pickstock and Ward, *Radical Orthodoxy: A New Theology*, 1.

# Bibliography

Augustine. *Confessions*. Translated by R.S. Pine-Coffin. London: Penguin, 1961.

Bainton, Roland. *Here I Stand: A Life of Martin Luther*. Nashville, TN: Abingdon, 1950.

Bendroth, Margaret. "What Wilt Thou Have Me To Do?" In *More Than Conquerors: Portraits of Believers from All Walks of Life*, edited by John Woodbridge, 336–39. London: Candle, 1992.

Berkhof, Louis. *Systematic Theology*. Edinburgh: Banner of Truth, 1939.

Bilinda, Lesley. *The Colour of Darkness*. London: Hodder & Stoughton, 1996.

Bishop, Jim. *The Day Christ Died*. London: Hodder & Stoughton, 1999.

Bly, Robert. *Iron John: A Book About Men*. Rockport, MA.: Element, 1990.

Boulay, Shirley, Du. *Tutu: Voice of the Voiceless*. London: Hodder & Stoughton, 1987.

Browning, Don. *A Fundamental Practical Theology*. Philadelphia: Fortress, 1991.

Bunyan, John. *Grace Abounding to the Chief of Sinners*. London: Penguin, 1987.

Campbell, Joseph. *The hero with a Thousand Faces*. 2nd Edition. Princeton: Princeton University Press, 1968.

Carvakho, Sarah, de. *The Street Children of Brazil: One Woman's Remarkable Story*. London: Hodder & Stoughton, 1996.

Colson, Charles. *Born Again: What Really Happened to the White House Hatchet Man* (London: Hodder & Stoughton, 1976.

Cooper, Brian. *Meeting Famous Christians*. Great Wakering: Mayhew-Mccrimmon, 1977.

Craig, Mary. *Six Modern Martyrs*. New York: Crossroad, 1984.

Davis, Willard. "Abraham Lincoln: Savior of a Nation." In *More Than Conquerors: Portraits of Believers from All Walks of Life*, edited by John Woodbridge, 14–21. London: Candle, 1992.

Demaus, Robert. *William Tindale*. London: Religious Tract Society, 1936.

Duffy, Eamon. *Unforgettable Fire: The Story of U2*. London: Penguin, 1987.

Frost, Brian. *Struggling to Forgive: Nelson Mandela and South Africa's Search for Reconciliation*. London: HarperCollins, 1998.

Gidney, Chris. *In the Limelight*. London: Marshall Pickering, 1993.

González-Balado, José Luis. *Always the Poor: Mother Teresa, Her Life and Message*. Liguori: Liguori Publications, 1980.

Graham, Billy, *Just as I Am*. London: Harper Collins, 1997.

Guinness, Michele. *The Guinness Legend*. London: Hodder & Stoughton, 1989.

Harrison, Ted. *Kriss Akabusi on Track: The Extraordinary Story of a Great Athlete* (Oxford: Lion, 1991.

Hatton, Jean. *Betsy: The Dramatic Biography of Prison Reformer Elizabeth Fry*. Oxford: Monarch, 2005.

Henriquez, José. *Miracle in the Mine: One Man's Story of Strength and Survival in the Chilean Mines*. Grand Rapids, MI: Zondervan, 2011.

Irvine, Doreen. *From Witchcraft to Christ*. London: Concordia, 1973.

Jacques, Elliott. "Death and the Mid-Life Crisis." *International Journal of Psychoanalysis* 46 (1965) 502–14.

John, J., and Marke Stibbe, *A Box of Delights*. London: Monarch, 2001.

Johnson, D.P. *Eric H. Liddell: Athlete and Missionary*. Crieff: The Research Unit, 1971.

Jung, C. *Psychological Reflections: a New Anthology of His Writings, 1905–1961*. Princeton University Press, 1973.

Kandell, Jonathan. "The Glorious History of Handel's Messiah," *Smithsonian Magazine* (Dec 2009). Accessed online 18 August 2016: http://www.smithsonianmag.com/arts-culture/the-glorious-history-of-handels-messiah-148168540/?no-ist

Kavanagh, Patrick. *The Spiritual Lives of Great Composers*. Milton Keynes: Word, 1992.

Kearney, R., *On Stories*. London: Routledge, 2002.

Kirkby, John. *Nevertheless*. Bradford: CAP Books, 2006.

Kushner, Harold. *When All You've Ever Wanted Isn't Enough*. New York: Pocket, 1986.

———. *When Bad Things Happen to Good People* (New York: Pocket, 1983.

Laloux, Frederic. *Reinventing Organizations: A guide to Creating Organizations Inspired by the Next Stage of Human Consciousness*. Brussels: Nelson Parker, 2014.

Lemon, Fred and Gladys Knowlton. *Breakout: A Violent Criminal Finds Christ*. London: Marshall, Morgan & Scott, 1977.

Lynch, Gordon. *Understanding Theology and Popular Culture*. Oxford Blackwell, 2005.

Meroff, Deborah. *True Grit: Women Taking on the World, for God's Sake*. Milton Keynes: Authentic, 2004.

Milbank, John. *Theology and Social Theory: Beyond Secular Reason*. Revised Edition. Oxford: Blackwell, 2006.

Milbank, John, Pickstock, Catherine and GrahamWard, *Radical Orthodoxy: A New Theology*. London: Routledge, 1999.

Muggeridge, Malcolm. *Something Beautiful for God*. London: HarperCollins, 1972.

Myers, John Brown. *William Carey*. Kilmarnock: John Ritchie, 1887.

O'Collins, Gerald. *The Second Journey: Spiritual Awareness and the Mid-Life Crisis*. Dublin: Villa, 1979.

Pappas, Stephanie. "To Hell and Back: How 69 Days Underground Affects Spirituality." *NBC News* (14 October 2010). Accessed online 18 August 2016: http://www.nbcnews.com/id/39658360/ns/health-behavior/#.V7b4_SgrLIU

Park, Jae-Eun. "Lacking Love or Conveying Love? The Fundamental Roots of the Donatists and Augustine's Nuanced Treatment of Them." *Reformed Theological Review* 72 (Aug 2013) 103–121.

Pauli, Hertha. *Handel and the Messiah Story*. New York: Meredith, 1968.

Pollock, John. *A Fistful of Heroes*. Basingstoke: Marshall Pickering, 1988.

———. *John Wesley*. Oxford: Lion, 1989.

———. *A Fistful of Heroes*. Revised Edition. Fearn: Christian Focus, 1998.

———. *Amazing Grace: John Newton's Story*. London: Hodder & Stoughton, 1981.

Pullinger Jackie & Andrew Quicke. *Chasing the Dragon*. London: Hodder & Stoughton, 1980.

Shapriro, Helen. *Walking Back to Happiness*. London: HarperCollins, 1993.

Shepperd, W.J. Limmer. *The Great Hymns and Their Stories*. Guildford: Lutterworth Press, 1979.

Squires, Sally. "Midlife Without a Crisis," *Washington Post* (April 19, 1999), Page Z20. Accessed online 25 August 2016: http://www.washingtonpost.com/wp-srv/health/seniors/stories/midlife042099.htm

Ten Boom, Corrie. *The Hiding Place*. Washington: Chosen Books, 1971.

Thayer, William. *Men Who Win, or, Making Things Happen*. London: T. Nelson, 1897.

Tinsley, E.J. (editor) *Dietrich Bonhoeffer*. London: Epworth Press.

Trench, Sally. *Bury Me in My Boots*. London: Hodder & Stoughton, 1999.

Vogler, Christopher. *The Writer's Journey: Mythic Structure for Writers*. 3rd Edition. Studio City, CA: Michael Wiese, 2007.

Whitaker, Colin. *Great Revivals*. Eastbourne: Kingsway, 2005.

———. *Seven Great Prayer Warriors*. Basingstoke: Marshall Pickering, 1987.

# Index of Heroes

www.ingramcontent.com/pod-product-compliance
Lightning Source LLC
Chambersburg PA
CBHW070500090426
42735CB00012B/2633